Dongliang Peng

An Optimization-Based Approach
for Continuous Map Generalization

Dongliang Peng

An Optimization-Based Approach
for Continuous Map Generalization

Würzburg
University Press

Dissertation, Julius-Maximilians-Universität Würzburg
Fakultät für Mathematik und Informatik, 2017
Gutachter: Prof. Dr. Alexander Wolff and Prof. Dr. Dirk Burghardt

Impressum

Julius-Maximilians-Universität Würzburg
Würzburg University Press
Universitätsbibliothek Würzburg
Am Hubland
D-97074 Würzburg
www.wup.uni-wuerzburg.de

© 2019 Würzburg University Press
Print on Demand

Coverdesign: Jule Petzold

ISBN 978-3-95826-104-4 (print)
ISBN 978-3-95826-105-1 (online)
DOI 10.25972/wup-978-3-95826-105-1
URN urn:nbn:de:bvb:20-opus-174427

Preface

In his thesis, Dongliang Peng investigates computational aspects of a fundamental problem in cartography called *generalization*. Cartographic generalization is the problem that has to be solved when producing a small-scale map (say, at scale 1 : 10,000) from data collected at a larger scale (say, 1 : 2,000). Traditionally, this has been a labor-intensive task that required highly-skilled cartographers with expertise in both geodesy and map-making. How should a row of ten houses be represented if the distances between them are too small to be represented correctly at the desired scale? By fewer, say, five houses? Or rather by a block of houses?

Dongliang attacks this and several other special cases of cartographic generalization in a modern setting. Think of online maps that users can (and want to!) zoom and pan with their finger tips. Other than traditional paper maps that were produced and printed for a fixed, small number of scales, online maps should ideally be available at *any* scale (within a reasonable interval). The problem of computing and displaying maps at arbitrary scales is called *continuous generalization*. Some aspects of continuous generalization (such as the example with the houses above) are inherently discrete, others (such as a wiggly river) can be treated more easily in a continuous fashion.

In several chapters of this thesis, Dongliang approaches continuous generalization problems in an innovative, yet formal way by using powerful tools from mathematical optimization such as integer linear programming. The main advantage of such an approach is that it helps to get the *model* right. Many problems can be cast into integer linear programs, which allows us to solve at least small examples to optimality—according to our model. If these solutions don't turn out as expected, we know that our model is wrong—not the algorithm. In contrast, when using only heuristics, solutions can come with errors of two types; those caused by the heuristic and those caused by the model. In this case, it is hard to understand and fix the errors.

In Chapter 2, Dongliang compares two potentially exact methods for the well-known area-aggregation problem. He asks for an optimal sequence of operations that aggregates, step-by-step, many "patches" of a detailed map into a single region of a coarser map. Dongliang uses a graph-based model in which he finds shortest paths (aka optimal aggregation sequences) using the A* algorithm and integer linear programming. The latter turns out to be much slower. He also compares the A* algorithm to an obvious greedy approach, which is surprisingly good given its simplicity. He also identifies a problem with his model.

Chapter 3 treats a related problem: how to best transit between two levels of administrative boundaries for zooming? The input consists of the two drawings at start and target scale, and the task is to mediate between the two in a continuous and topologically safe way. Dongliang finds the first topologically safe method of solving this problem based on *compatible triangulations* (a tool from computational geometry). Unfortunately, the existing algorithm for compatible triangulations sometimes introduces strong distortion locally. A way out may consist in choosing the Steiner points for the compatible triangulations more carefully, but this is left as an open problem.

In Chapter 4, Dongliang deals with the generalization of buildings. He shows how to generalize building footprints continuously such that well-defined blocks of buildings appear when the user of a digital map zooms out far enough. Here, only the building footprints are given. The approach animates a growing-process between the start scale and a target scale that can be set by the user. The algorithm computes a drawing for the target scale by a wisely chosen sequence of dilations and erosions (which have been used for building simplification before). In order to animate the growing-process in a continuous fashion, the buildings are expanded in a simple way: by moving their boundaries at constant speed and by clipping any part that leaves the target footprint. In order to guarantee a certain minimum distance between two buildings, the algorithm builds bridges between close-enough buildings. The computation of the bridges is based on a minimum spanning tree of the buildings. The resulting animations look very natural.

In Chapter 5, Dongliang explores an important subproblem that often appears in continuous generalization: how to "morph" a polygonal chain from a start to a target scale. He uses an existing algorithm to define a correspondence between the two chains and then computes trajectories for each pair of corresponding vertices. The aim is to find trajectories such that the angles and the edge lengths change in a uniform and continuous fashion—if possible. Dongliang applies least-squares adjustment in order to gradually move the chain from its start configuration to the target chain. While the results on real-world data look quite good, Dongliang also found artificial examples where self-intersection and numerical problems occur. Hence, least squares is probably not the ideal method for this problem.

Finally, in Chapter 6, Dongliang presents a case study to highlight the difficulties when working with geographic data naively. As a concrete example, he considers the problem of finding, in a set of n points in the plane, all pairs of points that are closer to each other than a given threshold ε. He compares three approaches for this problem, the text-book approach based on the sweep-line paradigm, a Delaunay-triangulation-based approach, and a simple grid-based approach. While the grid-based approach wins in terms of runtime, the different implementations of the sweep-line algorithms are what makes the comparison interesting—a lot depends on how the library methods are implemented, so the programmer should always read the fine print.

In his thesis, Dongliang exemplifies the optimization-based approach at various continuous generalization problems and demonstrates the strength of this approach. We see this as a very valuable contribution to GIScience where very all too often, problems are not modeled properly, and then algorithms are devised that happen to produce good-looking results on a small set of benchmark instances. We hope that many readers of this thesis will get inspired by Dongliang's way of tackling spatial problems!

Alexander Wolff (first supervisor)
Chair of Algorithms, Complexity and Knowledge-Based Systems
Faculty of Mathematics and Computer Science
University of Würzburg

Jan-Henrik Haunert (second supervisor)
Institute of Geodesy and Geoinformation
Faculty of Agriculture
University of Bonn

Abstract

Maps are the main tool to represent geographical information. Geographical information is usually scale-dependent, so users need to have access to maps at different scales. In our digital age, the access is realized by zooming. As discrete changes during the zooming tend to distract users, smooth changes are preferred. This is why some digital maps are trying to make the zooming as continuous as they can. The process of producing maps at different scales with smooth changes is called *continuous map generalization*.

In order to produce maps of high quality, cartographers often take into account additional requirements. These requirements are transferred to models in map generalization. Optimization for map generalization is important not only because it finds optimal solutions in the sense of the models, but also because it helps us to evaluate the quality of the models. Optimization, however, becomes more delicate when we deal with *continuous* map generalization. In this area, there are requirements not only for a specific map but also for relations between maps at difference scales. This thesis is about continuous map generalization based on optimization.

First, we show the background of our research topics. Second, we find optimal sequences for aggregating land-cover areas. We compare the A^* algorithm and integer linear programming in completing this task. Third, we continuously generalize county boundaries to provincial boundaries based on compatible triangulations. We morph between the two sets of boundaries, using dynamic programming to compute the correspondence. Fourth, we continuously generalize buildings to built-up areas by aggregating and growing. In this work, we group buildings with the help of a minimum spanning tree. Fifth, we define vertex trajectories that allow us to morph between polylines. We require that both the angles and the edge lengths change linearly over time. As it is impossible to fulfill all of these requirements simultaneously, we mediate between them using least-squares adjustment. Sixth, we discuss the performance of some commonly used data structures for a specific spatial problem. Last, we conclude this thesis and present open problems.

Zusammenfassung

Optimierung für die kontinuierliche Generalisierung von Landkarten

Landkarten sind das wichtigste Werkzeug zur Repräsentation geografischer Information. Unter der Generalisierung von Landkarten versteht man die Aufbereitung von geografischen Informationen aus detaillierten Daten zur Generierung von klein-maßstäbigen Karten. Nutzer von Online-Karten zoomen oft in eine Karte hinein oder aus einer Karte heraus, um mehr Details bzw. mehr Überblick zu bekommen. Die kontinuierliche Generalisierung von Landkarten versucht die Änderungen zwischen verschiedenen Maßstäben stetig zu machen. Dies ist wichtig, um Nutzern eine angenehme Zoom-Erfahrung zu bieten.

Um eine qualitativ hochwertige kontinuierliche Generalisierung zu erreichen, kann man wichtige Aspekte bei der Generierung von Online-Karten optimieren. In diesem Buch haben wir Optimierung bei der Generalisierung von Landnutzungskarten, von administrativen Grenzen, Gebäuden und Küstenlinien eingesetzt. Unsere Experimente zeigen, dass die kontinuierliche Generalisierung von Landkarten in der Tat von Optimierung profitiert.

Contents

Chapter 1

Introduction

Maps are the main tool to represent geographical information. As geographical information is usually scale-dependent [Mül+95; Wei97], users need to have access to maps at different scales. In order to generate these maps, national mapping agencies produce a base map and then derive maps at smaller scales by *map generalization*. More specifically, map generalization is the process of extracting and arranging geographical information from detailed data in order to produce maps at smaller scales. A requirement of map generalization is to emphasize the essential while suppress the unimportant, and at the same time maintain logical relationship between objects [Wei97]. As manual generalization is labor-intensive [Duc+14], automating map generalization is a promising way to produce up-to-date maps at high speed and low cost [MBD16].

In our digital age, people interactively read maps on computers and mobile phones. An often used interaction is zooming. When users zoom in or out, a map must be changed to provide information appropriate to the corresponding zoom level. However, large discrete changes may distract users. The *on-the-fly generalization* [WB17], which generalizes map features (e.g., polyglines and polygons) in real time, can mitigate this problem. Still, large discrete changes can be introduced. By a usability test, Midtbø and Nordvik [MN07] have shown that a map is easier to follow if the map extent transits smoothly than stepwise. In addition to smoothly transiting map extent, we want to change also map features smoothly when users are zooming. We believe that this strategy will allow users to follow maps even more easily. The process of producing maps at any different scales with smooth changes is known as *continuous map generalization* (CMG), or simply *continuous generalization*. Ideally, there should be no discrete change in CMG. However, the term is also used when the discrete changes are small enough not to be noticed as, e.g., Šuba et al. [ŠMO16] state.

1.1 State of the Art

1.1.1 Continuous Map Generalization

Continuous map generalization (CMG) has received a lot of attention from cartographers and computer scientists. Van Kreveld [Kre01] proposed five gradual changes to support the continuous zooming of maps, which are *moving, rotating, morphing, fading*, and *appearing*. He suggested using these gradual changes to adapt dis-

crete generalization operators for CMG. Sester and Brenner [SB05] suggested simplifying building footprints based on small incremental steps and to animate each
step smoothly. Li and Zhou [LZ12] built hierarchies of road segments, which they
then used to omit road segments from lower levels of the hierarchy. Moreover, they
evaluated similarities between their results and existing maps. Touya and Dumont
[TD17] progressively replaced buildings with blocks. In addition, their method automatically inferred landmarks and put the landmarks on top of the blocks. Šuba
et al. [ŠMO16] continuously generalized road networks which are represented as
a set of areas. Their method repeatedly finds the least-important area and then either merges it with an adjacent area or collapses it to a line segment. Danciger et
al. [Dan+09] investigated the growing of regions, while preserving topology, area
ratios, and relative positions. The strategy of using two maps at different scales to
generate intermediate-scale maps has been studied in multiple representations, e.g.,
with respect to the selection of roads or rivers [PDZ12; GT14]. Actually, this strategy
is the key idea of the morphing-based methods for CMG. In order to morph from
one polyline to another polyline, which respectively represent, say, roads on a larger-
scale map and a smaller-scale map, we first need to compute corresponding points
between them [e.g., Cec03; Nöl+08; Cha+10; DP15; LLX17; Li+17]. Then morphing can be realized by interpolating a set of intermediate polylines. Nöllenburg
et al. [Nöl+08] computed an optimum correspondence between two given polylines
according to some cost function. While straight-line trajectories are often used for
interpolation [e.g., Cec03; DP15], Whited and Rossignac [WR11] considered four
other alternatives, i.e., *hat, tangent, circular,* and *parabolic* paths based on so-called
ball-map [Cha+10]. Van Oosterom and Meijers [OM14] used a data structure called
smooth topological generalized area partitioning to support visualizing CMG. One of
their contributions is that a polygon is merged into another polygon continuously
by moving the boundary of the former. Huang et al. [Hua+17] proposed a matrix-
based structure to support CMG, using a river network as an example. For a given
scale, their structure yields the rivers that should be kept as well as how much these
rivers should be simplified.

1.1.2 Optimization in Map Generalization

Map generalization generally specifies and takes into account requirements in order
to produce maps of high quality [Sto+09a]. We categorize requirements as hard and
soft constraints. For example, when users zoom out, some land-cover areas become
too small to be seen. These areas need to be aggregated. When we aggregate one
area into another, the type of the former is changed to the type of the latter. In this
problem, a hard constraint could be that we aggregate only two polygons at each
step in order to keep changes small (see for example Figure 1.1). A soft constraint
could be that we wish to minimize the changes of types, e.g., we prefer aggregating
a grass area into a farm area rather than into a settlement area. This is a typical
optimization problem, where we stick to hard constraints and try to fulfill soft ones as

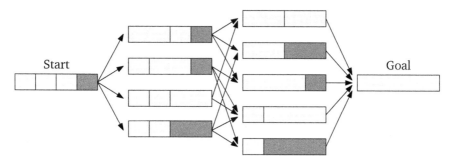

Figure 1.1: There are many ways of aggregating a set of land-cover areas to a single one.

well as possible. Optimization for map generalization is important not only because it finds optimal solutions, but also because it helps us to evaluate the quality of a model [HW17; HS08; HW16]. When we wish to minimize the changes of types in aggregating areas one by one, a model could be to minimize the *greatest* change over all the steps. Using a greedy algorithm, we can minimize the change at each step, but the result does not necessarily minimize the greatest change over all the steps. If a result is bad, we cannot tell if the bad result comes from the model or from the greedy algorithm. Using optimization, we are able to find optimal solutions of the model at least for small instances. If even an optimal solution is bad, then we can exclude that the bad result is from the greedy algorithm. That is to say, the bad result is because of the model. In this case, we should improve the model; we may want to minimize the *average* change over all the steps. Moreover, optimization is useful for evaluating heuristics. We need heuristics because many optimization problems cannot be solved efficiently [e.g., HW10a; HM16]. While heuristics can find some solutions in reasonable time, it is important to know the quality of these solutions. Fortunately, we can often find an optimal solution when the size of an instance is sufficiently small. Consequently, we are able to evaluate the quality of a heuristic by comparing its results with optimal solutions on small instances.

Optimization has been widely used in map generalization. For example, Harrie [Har99] displaced objects based on least-squares adjustments (LSA) to solve spatial conflicts. In his problem, the soft constraints for shapes and locations may contradict each other. Therefore, it is necessary to mediate between these constraints, which can be done by LSA. Sester [Ses05] used LSA not only for displacing objects but also for simplifying buildings. She required that the output boundaries should be as close to the original buildings as possible. Tong et al. [Ton+15] generalized land-cover areas, where LSA was used to preserve the sizes of the land-cover areas. Regnauld [Reg01] grouped buildings based on minimum spanning trees in order to typify the buildings in a group. Burghardt [Bur05] smoothed lines based on energy minimization. According to his setting, a line contains less energy if it is smooth and close to the original line. He repeatedly displaced the line until a stable state in terms of minimizing his energy function is found. Haunert and Wolff [HW10a]

aggregated land-cover areas based on mixed-integer linear programming to generate a map at a target scale. Their method is based on a global optimization. They
minimize a combination of type changes and cost for non-compact shapes while sat-
isfying constraints on the sizes of the output regions. Haunert and Wolff [HW10b]
simplified building footprints by solving an integer linear program (ILP). They aimed
at minimizing the number of edges in the output under the restriction that the simplified buildings must be topologically safe, that is, the selected and extended edges
must not intersect with each other. Oehrlein and Haunert [OH17] aggregated the
departments of France according to unemployment rates based on integer linear programming; they used a cutting-plane method to speed up solving their ILP. Funke
et al. [Fun+17] simplified administrative boundaries based on an ILP. Their aim was
to minimize the number of edges while keeping the result boundaries close to the
original ones and avoiding any intersection. At the same time, they required that
every city, represented by a point, stays in the same face as before the generalization.

1.1.3   Optimization in *Continuous* Map Generalization

Optimization becomes more delicate when we deal with CMG. In this field, we have
requirements not only for a specific map but also for relations between maps at
difference scales. Some optimization techniques have been applied to CMG. In the
aforementioned article, Nöllenburg et al. [Nöl+08] used dynamic programming to
match points of two polylines to support morphing according to some matching cost.
Schwartges et al. [Sch+13] used mixed-integer linear programming to select points
of interest. They required that a point, once disappeared, should not show up again
during zooming out. They also required that any two points should be sufficiently far
away from each other. Based on these requirements, they wanted to show as many
points as possible for a given scale interval. Chimani et al. [CDH14] computed a
deletion sequence for a road network by integer linear programming and efficient
approximation algorithms. They wanted to delete a stroke, which is a sequence of
edges, at each step while keeping the remaining network connected. They assigned
each edge a weight, and their objective was to maximize the total weight over all
the road networks of all the steps.

1.2   Tools for Optimization

In this thesis, we use some well-known optimization methods, namely, the A* algorithm [HNR68], integer linear programming [PS82, Chapter 13], dynamic program-
ing [Cor+09, Chapter 15], and least-squares adjustment (LSA) [Koc88, Chapter 3].
We also use the minimum spanning tree; see Cormen et al. [Cor+09, Chapter 23].
We use A* and integer linear programming to find optimal sequences for area aggregation (see Chapter 2). Similar to Nöllenburg et al. [Nöl+08], we use dynamic

programming to compute corresponding points between polylines (see Chapters 3 and 5). We use the minimum spanning tree to group buildings, which is similar to Regnauld [Reg01]; see Chapter 4. We define trajectories based on LSA for morphing between polylines (see Chapter 5). In the following, we briefly recall these methods.

1.2.1 The A* Algorithm

Given a graph with nodes and weighted edges, a typical task is to find a shortest path from a start node to a goal node. A breadth-first search [Cor+09, Chapter 22] solves the shortest-path problem in unweighted graphs. Dijkstra's algorithm [Dij59] always chooses from the explored nodes the neighbor with minimum distance from the start node. The A* algorithm is a generalized version of Dijkstra's algorithm. When A* chooses a node to explore the neighbors, the algorithm does not only take into account the distance from the start node but also estimates the distance to the goal node. By always choosing a node which is likely to be closer to the goal node, A* often explores fewer nodes than Dijkstra's algorithm in finding a shortest path. If the estimated distances are always smaller than the exact distances to the goal node, then A* will find a shortest path.

1.2.2 Integer Linear Programming

Linear programming models an optimization problem as objective functions subject to constraints, where the objective functions and constraints are represented by linear functions of some variables. These constraints form a convex polyhedron. An optimal solution lies on the boundary of the polyhedron and can be found efficiently. *Integer* linear programming requires that the variables must use integers. Integer linear programming is NP-hard since many NP-hard problems such as vertex cover can be formulated as integer linear programs. Intuitively, this is due to the fact that the optimal solution may lie in the interior of the polyhedron, where geometry does not help to find it. If only some of the variables are required to be integers (other variables are allowed to be non-integers), then the problem is called mixed integer linear programming, which is also known as NP-hard; see for more details Schrijver [Sch86, Chapter 16].

1.2.3 Dynamic Programming

Dynamic programming decomposes a big instance of a complex problem into a collection of smaller subinstances. The method solves each subinstance just once and saves the solution. The next time when the same subinstance occurs, the method will use the previously computed solution instead of resolving this subinstance. In this way, the method saves computation time. Other than in the divide-and-conquer approach used, e.g., in Mergesort, in dynamic programming subinstances of equal size are usually *not* disjoint but overlap.

1.2.4 Least-Squares Adjustment

Least-squares adjustment is a model for solving over-constrained problems. It handles computes a set of unknowns based on a set of observations. Because of errors, the observations may contradict each other. We have to adjust the observations so that we can obtain a set of unknowns that agree all the adjusted observations. There can be infinitely many sets of adjustments feasible, but we choose the one with the least sum of squared adjustments. Based on this set of adjustments, we can finally compute the unknowns.

1.2.5 Minimum Spanning Tree

Given a graph with nodes and weighted edges, a minimum spanning tree (MST) of the graph is a minimum-weight subset of the edges that together connect all nodes. Surprisingly, the MST can be computed by simple greedy algorithms such as Kruskal's algorithm [Kru56] or the algorithm of Jarník–Prim [Jar30; Pri57]. Strictly speaking, the MST by itself is not an optimization *method*, but it is a helpful structure of low weight that helps to solve many optimization problems in graph theory at least approximately, for example, the metric version of the famous Traveling Salesperson Problem (TSP).

1.3 Overview of the Thesis

This thesis contains five chapters that deal with methods for continuous map generalization. First, we find optimal sequences for aggregating land-cover areas. Second, we continuously generalize county boundaries to provincial boundaries. Third, we continuously generalize buildings to built-up areas by aggregating and growing. Fourth, we define moving trajectories based on least-squares adjustment for morphing between polylines. Fifth, we discuss the performance of data structures for spatial problems. In the remainder of this section, we present our results in more detail.

Finding Optimal Sequences for Area Aggregation—A* vs. Integer Linear Programming

To provide users with maps of different scales and to allow them to zoom in and out without losing context, automatic methods for map generalization are needed. We approach this problem for land-cover maps. Given two land-cover maps at two different scales, we want to find a sequence of small incremental changes that gradually transforms one map into the other. We assume that the two input maps consist of polygons each of which belongs to a given land-cover type. Every polygon on the smaller-scale map is the union of a set of adjacent polygons on the larger-scale map.

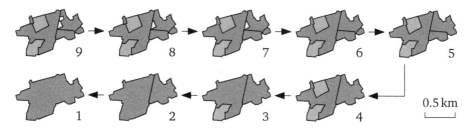

Figure 1.2: Some intermediate aggregation results of a region (Buchholz in der Nordheide, Germany). There are 9 polygons on the larger-scale map (top left). These areas are aggregated into one on the smaller-scale map (bottom left). The digits are the numbers of the areas.

In each step of the sequence that we compute, the smallest area is merged with one of its neighbors. We do not select that neighbor according to a prescribed rule but compute the whole sequence of pairwise merges at once, based on global optimization. We have proved that this problem is NP-hard. We formalize this optimization problem as that of finding a shortest path in a (very large) graph. We present the A* algorithm and integer linear programming to solve this optimization problem. To avoid long computing times, we allow the two methods to return non-optimal results. In addition, we present a greedy algorithm as a benchmark. We tested the three methods with a dataset of the official German topographic database ATKIS. Our main result is that A* finds optimal aggregation sequences for more instances than the other two methods within a given time frame. Figure 1.2 shows some intermediate results obtained by A* for one of the regions. This is joint work with Alexander Wolff and Jan-Hendrik Haunert, part of which has been published [see PWH17].

Continuously Generalizing Administrative Boundaries Based on Compatible Triangulations

Topological consistency is a key issue in cartographic generalization. Our aim in this chapter is to ensure topological consistency during continuous map generalization of administrative boundaries. To this end, we present a five-step method. Our inputs are two maps of administrative boundaries at different scales, where the larger-scale map has not only more details but also an additional level of administrative regions.

Our main contribution is the proposal of a workflow for generalizing hierarchical administrative boundaries in a continuous and topologically consistent way. First, we identify corresponding boundaries between the two maps. We call the remaining boundary pieces (on the larger-scale map) *unmatched* boundaries. Second, for the unmatched boundaries, we generate their corresponding boundaries on the smaller-scale map based on compatible triangulations. Third, we simplify the gener-

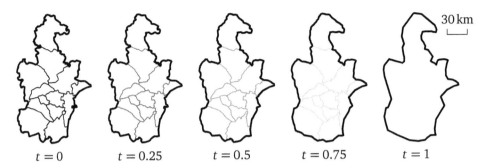

$t = 0$ $\qquad$ $t = 0.25$ $\qquad$ $t = 0.5$ $\qquad$ $t = 0.75$ $\qquad$ $t = 1$

Figure 1.3: Continuously generalizing county boundaries to provincial boundaries of Tianjin province, China.

ated boundaries by Douglas–Peukcer algorithm. Fourth, we compute corresponding points for each pair of corresponding boundaries using a variant of an existing dynamic programming algorithm. Fifth, we interpolate between the corresponding points to generate the boundaries at intermediate scales.

We do a thorough case study on the provincial and the county boundaries of Mainland China. Although topologically consistent algorithms for the third step and the fifth step exist, we have implemented simpler algorithms for our case study. Figure 1.3 shows our results of continuously generalizing county boundaries to provincial boundaries of Tianjin, China. This is joint work with Alexander Wolff and Jan-Hendrik Haunert [see PWH16].

Continuously Generalizing Buildings to Built-up Areas by Aggregating and Growing

To enable smooth zooming, we propose a method to continuously generalize buildings from a given start map to a smaller-scale goal map, where there are only built-up area polygons instead of individual building polygons (see Figure 1.4). We name the buildings on the start map *original buildings*. For an intermediate scale, we aggregate the original buildings that will become too close by adding bridges. We grow the (bridged) original buildings based on buffering and simplify the grown buildings. We take into account the shapes of the buildings on both the preceding map and the goal map to make sure that the buildings are always growing. The running time of our method is in $O(n^3)$, where n is the total number of edges overall the original buildings.

The advantages of our method are as follows. First, we grow the buildings continuously and, at the same time, simplify the grown buildings. Second, right angles of buildings are preserved during growing: the merged buildings still look like buildings. Third, the distances between buildings are always larger than a specified threshold. We do a case study to show the performances of our method. This is joint work with Guillaume Touya [see PT17].

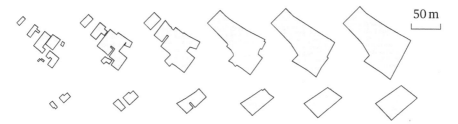

50 m

Figure 1.4: Continuously generalizing buildings to built-up areas by aggregating and growing.

Morphing Polylines Based on Least-Squares Adjustment

One way of continuously generalizing polylines is to use morphing techniques. Most often for morphing, the vertices of the polylines move on defined straight-line trajectories at constant speeds. In this chapter we address morphing of polylines, but we relax the requirement that the vertices of the polylines move on straight lines. Our concern with straight-line trajectories is that characteristic properties (e.g., bends) of the polylines change drastically during the morphing process. In particular, we suggest that the angles and the edge lengths of the polylines should change linearly during the morphing process. This expectation is clearly not accomplished with straight-line trajectories. In contrast, we present a new method based on least-squares adjustment that yields close-to-linear changes of the angles and the edge lengths. Figure 1.5 shows a comparison of morphing based on straight-line trajectories and our new morphing method. This is joint work with Jan-Henrik Haunert, Alexander Wolff, and Christophe Hurter [see Pen+13].

Choosing the Right Data Structures for Solving Spatial Problems

When we plan to implement a program, there are always many data structures that we can use to achieve a certain goal. However, if we do not carefully choose and use the data structures, the implemented program may be inefficient. As an example, we consider the problem of finding pairs of close points from a dataset. We consider two points to be close if they lie within a square of pre-specified side length ε. We compare three obvious algorithms to solve the problem: a sweep-line (SL) algorithm, an algorithm based on the Delaunay triangulation (DT) of the input points, and a hashing-like algorithm which overlays the input points with a rectangular grid. We implemented the algorithms in C# and tested them on randomly generated data and real-world data. We used the DT available in ArcGIS Objects. We used three different data structures of *balanced binary search* tree, i.e., SortedDictionary (SD), SortedSet (SS), and TreeSet (TS), to implement the sweep-line algorithm. The simple grid-based algorithm turned out to run faster than any of the other algorithms by a factor of at least 2 (see Figure 1.6). This is joint work with Alexander Wolff [see PW14].

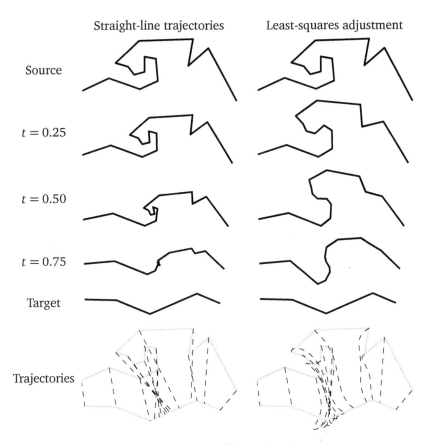

Figure 1.5: A comparison of morphing based on the two different trajectories.

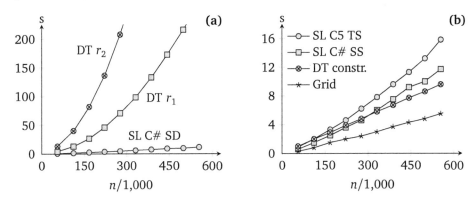

Figure 1.6: Time consumption of the algorithms for computing close point pairs. Two points are defined as close if the differences of their x- and y- coordinates are both smaller than $\varepsilon = 0.001267°$, where the coordinates are with unit degree. The DT-based algorithm took 262 s with radius $r_1 = \varepsilon \cdot (1 + \sqrt{2})/2$ ("DT r_1") and 784 s with radius $r_2 = \varepsilon \cdot (1 + \sqrt{7})/2$ ("DT r_2") for $n = 553{,}984$ points. The curve labeled "DT constr." represents the time for constructing Delaunay triangulations for the input points.

Chapter 2

Finding Optimal Sequences
for Area Aggregation—
A* vs. Integer Linear Programming

The land-cover area is of significant importance on maps. When users zoom out, some land-cover areas become too tiny to be seen, which result in visual clutter. In order to provide users with good visual experience during zooming operations, we propose to remove these tiny areas. We plan to achieve this goal by aggregating them into neighboring land-cover areas. A *land-cover map* is a planar subdivision in which each area belongs to a land-cover class or *type*. Suppose that there are two land-cover maps of different scales that cover the same spatial region. We consider the problem of finding a sequence of small incremental changes that gradually transforms the larger-scale map (the *start map*) to the smaller-scale map (the *goal map*). We use this sequence to generate and show land-cover maps at intermediate scales (see Figure 2.1). In this way, we try to avoid large and discrete changes during zooming.

With the same motivation, a strategy of hierarchical schemes has been proposed. This strategy generalizes a more-detailed representation to obtain a less-detailed representation based on small incremental changes, e.g., the Generalized Area Partitioning tree (GAP-tree). This tree can be constructed if only the larger-scale map is given [Oos05] or if both the larger-scale map and the smaller-scale map are given [HDO09]. Typically, the next change in such a sequence is determined locally, in a greedy fashion. If we insist on finding a sequence that is optimal according to some global measure, the problem becomes complicated.

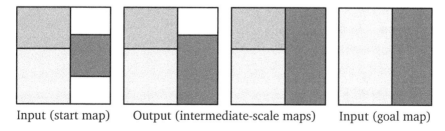

Input (start map) Output (intermediate-scale maps) Input (goal map)

Figure 2.1: The input and a possible output for an instance of our problem.

We assume that there exist many-to-one relationships between the areas of the start map and the areas of the goal map. This assumption is based on the fact that many algorithms [e.g., HW10a; Sma03; OH17] result in many-to-one relationships when aggregating land-cover areas. Their inputs and generalized results together can be used as our inputs. However, we should not use those algorithms to generate a sequence of maps at different scales because those algorithms do not take into account the consistence between the generated maps. We use both a start map and a goal map instead of using only the start map because our generated maps at intermediate scales should be able to benefit from a goal map with high quality. We term the areas of the goal map *regions*. That is, every region is the union of a set of areas on the start map. The type of a region may differ from the types of its components. For example, a small water area together with multiple adjacent forest areas may constitute a large forest region on the smaller-scale map. However, we assume that every region, on the goal map, contains at least one area of the same type on the start map. Our assumptions hold if the goal map has been produced with an automatic method for area aggregation, for example, by the method of Haunert and Wolff [HW10a]. That method produces a land-cover map at a single smaller scale, given a land-cover map at a larger scale. Although Haunert and Wolff [HW10a] attain results of high quality, they do not produce a sequence of land-cover maps.

Our method can also be extended to find an aggregation sequence for two maps (a start map and a goal map) that are from different sources. In that case, one could compute a map overlay of the two maps and use the result (with combined boundaries from both input maps and land cover classes from the given large-scale map) as the start map.

In this chapter, we try to find an optimal sequence to aggregate the land-cover areas on the start map one by one until we arrive at the goal map. We first independently deal with each region of the goal map (with its components on the start map). Once we have found an aggregation sequence for each region, we integrate all the sequences into an overall sequence, which transforms the start map into the goal map (see Figure 2.2). Our aggregation sequence may be cooperated with the GAP-face tree [Oos05], the map cube model [Tim98], or ScaleMaster [BB07; TG13], to support on-the-fly visualization. Smoothly (dis-)appearing areas can be realized by integrating our results into the *space-scale cube* [OM14; Oos+14].

Contribution. We formally model our problem, analyze the size of our model in a worst-case scenario, introduce our methods, and present the basic concepts of our method (Section 2.1). We define our cost functions (Section 2.2). We prove that our problem is NP-hard (Section 2.3). Then, we develop and compare three methods for finding aggregation sequences. First, we present a greedy algorithm (Section 2.4). Second, we develop a new global optimization approach based on the A* algorithm (Section 2.5). Third, we model our pathfinding problem as an *integer linear program* (ILP), and we solve this ILP with minimizing our cost function

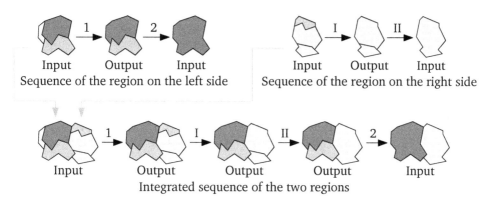

Figure 2.2: Integrating two aggregation sequences of different regions: the resulting sequence contains the given sequences as subsequences and always takes the subdivision with smallest patch next. The gray arrows show the integration of the two regions.

(Section 2.6). Our ILP uses binary (0–1) variables. These variables help us to model our problem, but in general, it is NP-hard to solve an ILP optimally. By comparing with the greedy algorithm, which is used as a benchmark, we are able to see whether A* or the ILP-based algorithm, which are more complex and slower, indeed perform better. Our case study uses a dataset of the German topographic database ATKIS (Section 2.7). In the concluding remarks, we show possible ways to improve our methods (Section 2.8).

We do not deal with simplifying polylines in this chapter. The simplification can be handled separately from the aggregation of areas by using one of the existing methods [e.g., DP73; Saa99; WSM04]. Those methods can be used to set up the binary line generalisation tree (BLG-tree) of van Oosterom and Schenkelaars [OS95], which is a hierarchical data structure that defines a gradual line simplification process. Although splitting polygons is a good step of generalizing land-cover areas, we do not integrate it into our method at this moment. Some examples of splitting are as follows. Smith et al. [Smi+07] and Thiemann and Sester [TS18] proposed to split tiny polygons and then to merge the split parts into the neighboring polygons. Meijers et al. [MSO16] developed an algorithm to split a polygon (the splittee) based on a constrained Delaunay triangulation. During splitting, their algorithm is capable of taking into account the attractivenesses between the splittee and its neighbors. When merging, a more attractive neighbor will get a larger portion from the splittee.

2.1 Preliminaries

We show how to compute an aggregation sequence for a single region, R. For a goal map with many regions, we "interleave" the sequences for each of them with respect to the order of the smallest patches (see for example Figure 2.2). This integration is similar to the merge step in the Mergesort algorithm; see Cormen et al. [Cor+09,

Section 2.3]. To allow us to describe our method more easily, below we assume that the goal map has only one region. This region consists of n land-cover areas (components) on the start map. In other words, the union of the n land-cover areas is the only region on the goal map.

To find a sequence of small changes that transforms the start map into the goal map, we require that every change involves only two areas of the current map. More precisely, in each step the smallest area u is merged with one of its neighbors v (v does not have to be the smallest neighbor) such that u and v are replaced by their union. The type of the union is restricted to be the type of either u or v. If the union uses the type of u, we say that area v is *aggregated into* area u, and vice versa. How to aggregate exactly is decided by optimizing a global cost function (see Section 2.2). This requirement ensures that the size of the smallest area on the map increases in each step. Hence, the sequence reflects a gradual reduction of the map's scale. From another perspective, we consider the smallest area as the least important, rather than involving more rules for (non-)importance. Even though the requirement reduces the number of possible solutions, there is still enough room for optimization since we leave open with which of its neighbors the smallest area is aggregated. We term a sequence of changes that adheres to our smallest-first requirement simply an *aggregation sequence*.

2.1.1 Model

We consider a directed graph G_S, which we call the *subdivision graph* (see Figure 2.3). The node set V_S of G_S contains nodes for all the possible maps (or *subdivisions*), including the start map, all possible intermediate-scale maps, and the goal map. The arc set E_S of G_S contains an arc $(P_{t,i}, P_{t+1,j})$ between any two maps $P_{t,i}$ and $P_{t+1,j}$ in V_S if $P_{t+1,j}$ can be reached from $P_{t,i}$ with a single aggregation operation, involving a smallest area. On this basis, any directed path in G_S from the start map to the goal map defines a possible aggregation sequence.

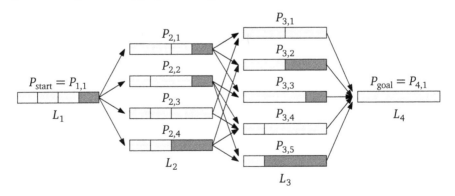

Figure 2.3: The subdivision graph, G_S. The nodes of the graph are the subdivisions. There is an arc from subdivision $P_{t,i}$ to subdivision $P_{t+1,j}$ if $P_{t+1,j}$ is the result of an aggregation step from $P_{t,i}$.

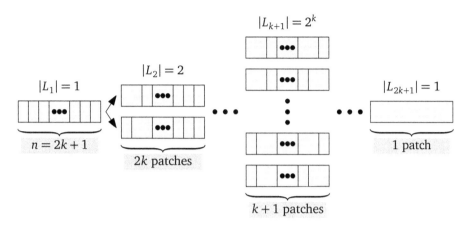

Figure 2.4: An example to show that the size of subdivision graph G_S has exponential lower bound.

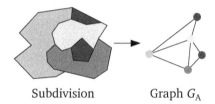

Subdivision   Graph G_A

Figure 2.5: The adjacency graph of a subdivision, G_A. Each polygon of the subdivision is represented as a node in the graph. There is an edge between two nodes if the corresponding two polygons are adjacent.

2.1.2 Notation

We represent each land-cover area by a polygon with a type. We denote by P the set of polygons on the start map. We use p, q, r, or o to denote polygons. A *patch* is a set of polygons whose union is connected. Each patch also has a unique land-cover type. We use u or v to denote the patches.

Recall that we are dealing with a single region and there are n land-cover areas on the start map in this region. Hence, the desired aggregation sequence consists of $n-1$ steps. There are n subdivisions on a path from the start map to the goal map. We use $t \in T = \{1, 2, \ldots, n\}$ to denote *time*. When $t = 1$, the subdivision consists of n patches, and there is only one patch remaining when $t = n$. The subdivision graph consists of layers $L_1, \ldots, L_n$, where layer $L_t = \{P_{t,1}, \ldots, P_{t,n_t}\}$ contains every possible subdivision $P_{t,i}$ with $n-t+1$ patches (see Figure 2.4).

Sometimes, we need a graph to represent the adjacencies of the land-cover areas in a subdivision, we call such a graph G_A (see Figure 2.5).

2.1.3 Exponential Lower Bound

We now analyze the size of subdivision graph G_S. Our analysis is inspired by Keane [Kea75], where we also use a row of n land-cover areas. In our instance (see Figure 2.4), the start map consists of $n = 2k + 1$ rectangular patches, and the goal map is simply the union of the n patches. The patches have area sizes $100 + \frac{1}{n}, 99 + \frac{2}{n}, 100 + \frac{3}{n}, 99 + \frac{4}{n}, \ldots, 99 + \frac{n-1}{n}$, and 101, from left to right. According to our setting, we always aggregate the smallest patch with one of its neighbors. Therefore, in the first k steps from the start map, we aggregate every other patch with one of its neighbors. However, we do not know which one is the right choice at each of the steps in order to minimize our costs (see Section 2.2). We have to try both of the two choices, aggregating with the left patch or with the right one. As a result, there are $2^k = 2^{(n-1)/2}$ subdivisions in layer L_{k+1}. That is to say, the size of subdivision graph G_S has exponential lower bound.

2.1.4 Methods

Our idea is to obtain an optimal aggregation sequence through computing a path with minimum weight, from the start to the goal (see Figure 2.3). This idea obviously requires that the arc weights are set; then we try to find a minimum-weight start–goal path that does actually correspond to an aggregation sequence of maximum cartographic quality. Putting the idea to practice is far from trivial since graph G_S can be huge. We compare a greedy algorithm, A*, and an ILP-based algorithm in finding such paths. Note that our inputs are only subdivisions P_{start} and P_{goal} (see Figure 2.3). We generate a subdivision (node) only when we want to visit it.

In directed acyclic graphs, shortest paths can be found slightly faster than in general directed or undirected graphs. An off-the-shelf shortest-path algorithm for directed acyclic graphs (e.g., Cormen et al. [Cor+09, Section 25.2]), however, will explore the whole graph, which has exponential size. Dijkstra's algorithm [Dij59], for a user-specified given source, computes shortest paths to all other nodes in an edge-weighted graph. Dijkstra's algorithm need to explore a large number of nodes even when computing only a single shortest path to a user-specified destination. The same holds for shortest-path algorithms that make use of a topological order of the nodes in a directed acyclic graph. Compared to these algorithms, the A* algorithm can greatly reduce the number of explored nodes. The challenge in our work was to tune the A* algorithm such that it explores only a small fraction of the graph.

2.2 Cost Functions

Figure 2.3 shows that there are many ways to aggregate from the start map to the goal map. Apparently, some of the ways are more reasonable than others. In our example, we consider sequence $(P_{1,1}, P_{2,1}, P_{3,1}, P_{4,1})$ more reasonable than sequence $(P_{1,1}, P_{2,4}, P_{3,5}, P_{4,1})$. This is because that the dark area should not expand so

much when the target color is light gray. We want to provide users with a most reasonable sequence because we believe that an unreasonable sequence irritates users.
To find a most reasonable sequence, we introduce cost functions. In the cost functions, we charge a higher penalty when an aggregation step is less reasonable. As
a result, by minimizing the overall cost of an aggregation sequence, we find a most
reasonable sequence.

It is difficult to define what *reasonable* exactly means because users may have
different preferences. Four preferences have been discussed by Cheng and Li [CL06];
see Figure 2.6. A small land-cover area can be aggregated into another area that
isolates the area (Figure 2.6b), that is the largest neighbor (Figure 2.6c), that shares
the longest boundary (Figure 2.6d), or that has the most similar type (Figure 2.6e).
To keep our aggregation problem independent of user preferences, our cost function
takes two aspects into account: one based on semantics and the other based on
shape. In terms of semantics, we require that the *type* of a land-cover area changes as
little as possible. This requirement means that we prefer, for example, aggregating
an area with type *swamp* into an area with type *wet ground* rather than into an
area with type *city*. In terms of shape, we hope to have areas which are as *compact*
as possible. Our argument is that an area is easier to be identified by a human
being if it is more compact (less clutter). We also consider the total *length* of the
interior boundaries as an alternative compactness; we consider subdivision $P_{t,i}$ as
more compact than subdivision $P_{t,i'}$ if the total length of the interior boundaries
of $P_{t,i}$ is less than that of $P_{t,i'}$. We add this alternative because we want to make a
comparison involving an ILP, where a *linear* cost function must be used. Note that
most compactness measures are *not* linear; for example, see Maceachren [Mac85]
and Li et al. [LGC13]. Although the length of interior boundaries is not sufficiently
precise to describe compactness [You88], it is often used as a fair alternative when
compactness is considered in an ILP [e.g., MH16; WRC83]. Haunert and Wolff
[HW10a] employed the centroids of a set of land-cover areas. One of their costs is
the sum of the distances from the centroids to a *reference point*. The reference point
is one of the centroids that minimizes the sum. The sum of the distances can be
computed linearly. We use the length of interior boundaries instead of the distance
of centroids because the former is more relevant to the shapes of the patches. Also,
Harrie et al. [HSD15] showed that longer lines generally yield lower map readability.

2.2.1 Cost of Type Change

Suppose that we are at the step of aggregating from subdivision $P_{s,i}$ to subdivision $P_{s+1,j}$. In this step, patch u is aggregated into patch v (see Figures 2.7a and
2.7b). We denote the types of the two patches by $T(u)$ and $T(v)$. We define the cost
of type change of this step by

$$f_{type}(P_{s,i}, P_{s+1,j}) = \frac{A_u}{A_R} \cdot \frac{d_{type}(T(u), T(v))}{d_{type\_max}}, \qquad (2.1)$$

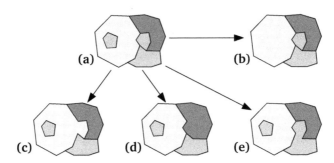

Figure 2.6: Aggregating land-cover areas according to different preferences by Cheng and Li [CL06]. Aggregating a small land-cover area into another one that isolates the area (b), that is the largest neighbor (c), that shares the longest boundary (d), or that has the most similar type (e).

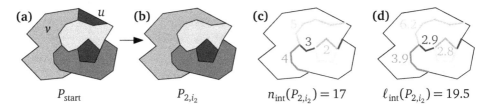

Figure 2.7: An aggregation step, where patch u is aggregated into patch v; see Figures (a) and (b). Figures (c) and (d) respectively show the number of edges and the lengths of the interior polylines after the aggregation.

where A_u is the area of patch u, and A_R is the area of region R (see Section 2.1). We use A_R and $d_{\text{type\_max}}$ to normalize the cost of type change. Constant $d_{\text{type\_max}}$, the maximum cost over all type changes, is known from the input. The input specifies cost $d_{\text{type}}(T_1, T_2)$ of changing type T_1 to type T_2. Specifically, we denote by T_{goal} the type of the patch on the goal map. For simplicity, we use a metric as the cost function of type change (see Section 2.7). A metric distance is symmetric, which is different from the asymmetric one used in Dilo et al. [DOH09]. In their definition, for example, the distance from type *building* to type *road* is 0.5, but the distance from *road* to *building* is 0.

For path $\Pi = (P_{1,i_1}, P_{2,i_2}, \ldots, P_{t,i_t})$, we define the cost of type change over the steps by

$$g_{\text{type}}(\Pi) = \sum_{s=1}^{t-1} f_{\text{type}}(P_{s,i_s}, P_{s+1,i_{s+1}}). \tag{2.2}$$

2.2.2 Cost of Compactness

We use the compactness definition of Frolov [Fro75], i.e., the compactness value of a patch, say, u is

$$c(u) = \frac{2\sqrt{\pi A_u}}{l_u}, \tag{2.3}$$

where A_u and l_u are the area and the perimeter. For subdivision $P_{s,i}$, we denote by $C(P_{s,i})$ the set of the patches' compactness values.

We wish to maximize the sum of the average compactness values over all intermediate maps, while our objective will be minimizing a cost function. To adapt the average compactness to our methods, we define and minimize a cost related to compactness. Recalling that there are $n - s + 1$ patches at time s, we define the cost of compactness for subdivision $P_{s,i}$ as

$$f_{\text{comp}}(P_{s,i}) = \frac{1 - \frac{1}{n-s+1}\sum_{c \in C(P_{s,i})} c}{n - 2}, \tag{2.4}$$

where we use values $n - s + 1$ and $n - 2$ to normalize the cost of compactness.

For path Π (see Section 2.2.1), we define the cost of compactness over all intermediate maps (that is, neglecting $P_{1,1}$ and the last subdivision in the path) by

$$g_{\text{comp}}(\Pi) = \sum_{s=2}^{t-1} f_{\text{comp}}(P_{s,i_s}). \tag{2.5}$$

2.2.3 Cost of Length

We denote the set of interior boundaries for a subdivision $P_{s,i}$ by $B(P_{s,i})$. The cost in terms of interior length of this subdivision is defined as

$$f_{\text{lgth}}(P_{s,i}) = \frac{\left(\sum_{b \in B(P_{s,i})} |b|\right)/D(s)}{n - 2}, \tag{2.6}$$

where

$$D(s) = \frac{n-s}{n-1} \sum_{b \in B(P_{\text{start}})} |b|. \tag{2.7}$$

Function $D(s)$ computes the "expected" total length of the interior boundaries at time s, where we expect that this total length decreases linearly according to time s. In special, $D(1) = \sum_{b \in B(P_{\text{start}})} |b|$ and $D(n) = 0$. Similarly to Equation 2.4, we use $D(s)$ and $n - 2$ to normalize the cost of length.

For path Π (see Section 2.2.1), we define the cost of length over all intermediate maps (that is, neglecting $P_{1,1}$ and the last subdivision in the path) by

$$g_{\text{lgth}}(\Pi) = \sum_{s=2}^{t-1} f_{\text{lgth}}(P_{s,i_s}). \tag{2.8}$$

Note that in theory, a patch, u, with a small perimeter can be extremely non-compact according to measure $c(u)$ in Equation 2.3, thus the two measures, f_{comp} and f_{lgth}, are not interchangeable. However, if we assume that all areas of the map have the same size (i.e., A_u of Equation 2.3 is a constant), it would make no difference whether we minimize an area's perimeter or maximize the area's compactness $c(u)$. Obviously, the areas in our dataset have different sizes. However, since we iteratively remove the smallest area, the differences do not become too large. Therefore, measuring the overall compactness of a map based on the total length of all the interior boundaries is quite reasonable.

2.2.4 Combining Cost Functions

When we generate a sequence of intermediate-scale maps, we want to change the types of the land-cover areas as little as possible and want to have compact land-cover areas. Therefore, we combine the cost of type change (Equation 2.2) and the cost of compactness (Equation 2.5). That is,

$$g_1(\Pi) = (1-\lambda)g_{\text{type}}(\Pi) + \lambda g_{\text{comp}}(\Pi), \tag{2.9}$$

where $\lambda \in [0,1]$ is a parameter to assign importances of f_{type} and f_{comp}. We simply use $\lambda = 0.5$ in our experiments. We want to find a path Π from P_{start} to $P_{t,i}$ that minimizes, among all such paths, $g_1(\Pi)$. Slightly abusing notation, we denote the cost of an optimal path from P_{start} to $P_{t,i}$ by $g_1(P_{t,i})$. Using $g_1(P_{t,i})$, we compare a greedy algorithm and A* in finding optimal sequences for area aggregation.

As said before, we want to make a comparison involving integer linear programming while our cost of compactness (see Equation 2.3) cannot be computed linearly in an integer linear program. Therefore, we combine the cost of type change (Equation 2.2) and the cost of length (Equation 2.8), which can be computed linearly in an integer linear program. That is,

$$g_2(\Pi) = (1-\lambda)g_{\text{type}}(\Pi) + \lambda g_{\text{lgth}}(\Pi). \tag{2.10}$$

We compare the greedy algorithm, A*, and an ILP-based algorithm using g_2.

2.3 NP-hardness Proof

Although we have shown that the graph of subdivisions has an exponential size (see Section 2.1), one may develop a clever algorithm to find an optimal sequence efficiently. In the following, we prove that finding such a sequence is indeed NP-hard. In the proof, we neglect the cost of compactness or the cost of length. Considering one of the two costs will make the computation even more difficult.

Theorem 1. AREAAGGREGATIONSEQUENCE is NP-hard even if we only consider the cost of type change.

Proof. Our NP-hardness proof is by reduction from the NP-complete problem PLANARVERTEXCOVER, which is to decide, for a given planar graph $G_A = (V_A, E_A)$, whether there exists a vertex cover with at most a given number k_A of vertices. For an instance of PLANARVERTEXCOVER (Figure 2.8a), we define a corresponding instance

PLANARVERTEXCOVER   AREAAGGREGATIONSEQUENCE

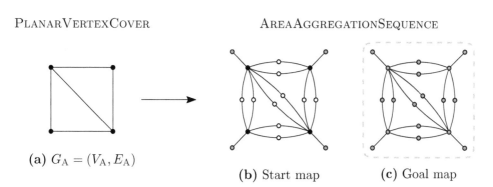

(a) $G_A = (V_A, E_A)$

(b) Start map   (c) Goal map

Figure 2.8: The reduction for our NP-hardness proof. The dashed polygon in (c) shows the merged vertices.

of AREAAGGREGATIONSEQUENCE whose start map consists of gray, black, and white areas and whose goal map consists of only one large gray patch. The adjacency graphs of the two maps are illustrated in Figures 2.8b and 2.8c, where the colors of the vertices represent the colors of the corresponding areas. More precisely, for each vertex of G_A in Figure 2.8a, we define a gray vertex and a black vertex, which we connect with an edge. For each edge $\{u, v\}$ of G_A, we define two white vertices and connect each of them both with the black vertex for u and the black vertex for v (Figure 2.8b).

We define the weights of the vertices in Figure 2.8b as follows:

- Every white vertex has weight 1.
- Every black vertex has weight 2.
- Every gray vertex has weight $2|V_A| + 2|E_A|$, which is equal to the total weight of all white and black vertices.

When we merge two vertices, the weight of the new vertex is the sum of the two. In each aggregation step, we require the smallest area to be aggregated with one of its neighbors. The area sizes correspond to the weights of the vertices in Figure 2.8b. Therefore, our definition of the weights to a certain degree determines the order in which the vertices are selected:

- *Phase I*: In each of the first $2|E_A|$ steps, a white vertex is selected and merged with one of its neighbors, such that the white vertex receives the neighbor's color or vice versa (Figure 2.9 shows a possible result).
- *Phase II*: In each of the next $|V_A|$ steps, a non-gray vertex is selected and merged with one of its neighbors.
- *Phase III*: $|V_A| - 1$ steps remain to reach the goal map.

To complete the reduction, we need to define the costs of color changes. For any color change, we charge one unit of cost per unit weight. Due to our construction, Phases II and III can be accomplished with a total cost of $2|V_A| + 2|E_A|$, no matter how Phase I is accomplished. This is because, after Phase I, every non-gray patch will be adjacent to a gray patch (vertex). Thus, if any non-gray patch becomes selected in Phase II, it can be aggregated with a gray patch (vertex) and receive the

Figure 2.9: The situation after Phase I has been conducted such that all black vertices corresponding to a vertex cover of G_A have been recolored white. The dashed polygons show that the vertices are merged.

color gray. This implies that Phase II costs $2|V_A| + 2|E_A|$ (which is equal to the total weight of all initially white and black vertices) and, since after Phase II all patches are gray, Phase III does not cause any additional cost. It is also clear that there is no cheaper way to accomplish Phases II and III, since it is impossible to color a vertex gray in Phase I. Consequently, since the total cost of Phases II and III is fixed, it is only interesting to ask at which cost Phase I can be accomplished. It turns out that, if G_A has a vertex cover $C_A \subseteq V_A$, then Phase I can be accomplished with cost $2|C_A|$; only the black vertices corresponding to vertices in C_A need to change their color from black to white, and each of them has weight 2 (see Figure 2.9). To summarize, if graph G_A has a vertex cover C_A, then the corresponding instance of AREAAGGREGATIONSEQUENCE has a solution of total cost $2|C_A| + 2|V_A| + 2|E_A|$.

It remains to be shown that, if C_A^* is a minimum vertex cover of G_A, then there is no solution with total cost less than $2|C_A^*| + 2|V_A| + 2|E_A|$. To see why, we assume that such a solution exists. If we keep the black color of a vertex from C_A^* (the total cost decreases by 2), then we will need to at least change two white vertices to black vertices (the total cost increases by 2 at least). Therefore, we have found a contradiction to our assumption.

$\square$

2.4 A Greedy Algorithm

A motivation for the greedy algorithm is that a very similar iterative algorithm has been used by van Oosterom [Oos05] for constructing the tGAP data structure. However, we have to make minor modifications to ensure that the computed aggregation sequence ends with the goal map that, in our situation, is given as a part of the input. We use our greedy algorithm as a benchmark so that we are able to see whether the A^* algorithm or the ILP-based algorithm indeed perform better.

At any time t, our greedy algorithm aggregates the smallest patch with one of its neighbors. We pick the neighbor in a greedy way. We suppose that the smallest patch, u, has k_u neighbors, then there are $2k_u$ ways to aggregate (when we aggregate a patch into another patch, the union uses the type of the latter). In order to guarantee that our final result (e.g., the polygon of layer L_4 in Figure 2.3) will have the type of T_{goal}, we add one more rule to our greedy algorithm. Suppose that patch v is one of u's neighbors. The greedy algorithm aggregates u into v if the type distances fulfill that $d_{\text{type}}\left(T(u), T_{\text{goal}}\right) \geq d_{\text{type}}\left(T(v), T_{\text{goal}}\right)$; otherwise, the algorithm aggregates v into u. This rule excludes, say, k_e aggregation choices, and we have $2k_u - k_e$ choices left. Then we compute the costs for each of the $2k_u - k_e$ aggregation choices and select the aggregation that has the least cost. In other words, we aggregate the smallest patch with its most *compatible* neighbor.

In accordance with our two combinatorial costs in Section 2.2.4, we define two cost functions. Suppose that we are at the step of aggregating from subdivision $P_{s,i}$ to subdivision $P_{s+1,j}$. The first cost function is

$$f_1(P_{s,i}, P_{s+1,j}) = (1-\lambda)f_{\text{type}}(P_{s,i}, P_{s+1,j}) + \lambda f_{\text{comp}}(P_{s+1,j}). \qquad (2.11)$$

The second cost function is

$$f_2(P_{s,i}, P_{s+1,j}) = (1-\lambda)f_{\text{type}}(P_{s,i}, P_{s+1,j}) + \lambda f_{\text{lgth}}(P_{s+1,j}). \qquad (2.12)$$

We take one of the $2k_u - k_e$ aggregation choices according to Equations 2.11 or 2.12 in our two experiments. The cost of a whole sequence can be computed by Equations 2.9 or 2.10.

2.5 Using the A* Algorithm

Section 2.1 has shown that the size of finding an optimal aggregation sequence can be exponential. That is to say, the graph G_S—our search space—can be of exponential size. In order to avoid computing the whole graph explicitly, we use the A* algorithm [HNR68; Pat]. To save time and memory, we generate a subdivision, $P_{t,i}$, only when we are going to visit it. A* uses a clever best-first search to find a shortest path from subdivision P_{start} to subdivision P_{goal}. For $P_{t,i}$, A* considers the exact cost of a shortest path from P_{start} to $P_{t,i}$ and estimates the cost to get from $P_{t,i}$ to P_{goal}. A* explores the nodes earlier if they are estimated to be closer to the goal. A* can be seen as a refinement of Dijkstra's algorithm [Dij59].

We define $g(P_{t,i})$ to be the exact cost of a shortest path from P_{start} to $P_{t,i}$ and define $h(P_{t,i})$ to be the estimated cost to get from $P_{t,i}$ to P_{goal}. Then, the (estimated) total cost at node $P_{t,i}$ is

$$F(P_{t,i}) = g(P_{t,i}) + h(P_{t,i}). \qquad (2.13)$$

We use either g_1 (Equation 2.9) or g_2 (Equation 2.10) for $g(P_{t,i})$; accordingly, we use either h_1 (Equation 2.23) or h_2 (Equation 2.24) for $h(P_{t,i})$. If $h(P_{t,i})$ is always bounded from above by the exact cost of a shortest path from $P_{t,i}$ to P_{goal}, A* guarantees to find a shortest path from P_{start} to P_{goal}, that is, an optimal aggregation sequence. Using estimate F (Equation 2.13), A* is able to reduce the search space. The better the estimation part h, the more search space A* can reduce. In the following, we show how to compute estimated cost $h(P_{t,i})$.

To narrow down the search space, we set up estimation functions for type change (Section 2.5.1), compactness (Section 2.5.2), and length (Section 2.5.3). These functions are meant to direct A* towards the goal. Since the number of subdivisions can be exponential, we may run out of the main memory before we find an optimal solution. To handle this problem, we introduce overestimations to find a feasible solution. Overestimations are popular when people cannot find optimal solutions using A*. For example, Pohl [Poh73] overestimated using dynamic weighting. We propose another strategy that fits our problem. We first try finding an optimal solution by A*. If we fail to find one after we have visited a predefined number, say, W of nodes of graph G_S, then we restart. In the retrying, we overestimate the first K steps starting at each node (see Sections 2.5.1, 2.5.2, and 2.5.3). We may need to increase K and retry several times until we find a feasible solution. Because we do not want to retry too many times, we define K by

$$K = 2^k - 1, \tag{2.14}$$

where $k \geq 0$ is the number of retryings. When $k = 0$, we have $K = 0$, which means that the first attempt of finding a solution does not use overestimation. As $K \leq n-1$, it holds that $k \leq \log_2 n$, which means that we need to retry $\lceil \log_2 n \rceil$ times at most. Whenever overestimating ($k \geq 1$), A* cannot guarantee optimality anymore. When we are at time t, there are at most $n - t$ steps to arrive at the goal map. We define the number of practical overestimation steps as

$$K' = \min\{K, n-t\}. \tag{2.15}$$

2.5.1 Estimating the Cost of Type Change

To find a lower bound of the cost of type change, we simply assume that every patch will be aggregated into a patch with type T_{goal}. As long as the cost of type change is a metric, this aggregation strategy indeed yields a lower bound. For subdivision $P_{t,i}$, let $(P_{t,i} = P_{t,i'_t}, P_{t+1,i'_{t+1}} \ldots, P_{n,i'_n} = P_{\text{goal}})$, be the path that always changes the type of a smallest patch to T_{goal}. Then the estimated cost of type change is

$$h_{\text{type}}(P_{t,i}) = \sum_{s=t}^{n-1} f_{\text{type}}(P_{s,i'_s}, P_{s+1,i'_{s+1}}). \tag{2.16}$$

As an example, for Figure 2.7b, we compute h_{type} according to the "aggregation sequence" of Figure 2.10. Note that the step from subdivision P_{2,i'_2} to subdivision P_{3,i'_3} in Figure 2.10 is impossible in reality because the dark patch cannot be aggregated into patch v as they are not neighbors. However, this aggregation is allowed for estimation because we may find a shortest path as long as the estimated cost is no more than the exact cost of a shortest path. When we need to overestimate,

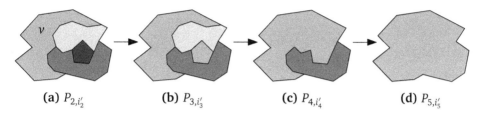

(a) $P_{2,i_2'}$ (b) $P_{3,i_3'}$ (c) $P_{4,i_4'}$ (d) $P_{5,i_5'}$

Figure 2.10: An "aggregation sequence" for computing the estimated cost of type change h_{type} (see Equations 2.16 and 2.17), based on the aggregation result of Figure 2.7b. Note that this aggregation sequence is impossible in reality, but it is fine for estimating (see the argument in Section 2.5.1).

we multiply the estimated cost of the first K' steps (see Equation 2.15) by K (see Equation 2.14). As a result, Formula 2.16 is revised to

$$h_{\text{type}}(P_{t,i}) = K \sum_{s=t}^{t+K'-1} f_{\text{type}}(P_{s,i_s'}, P_{s+1,i_{s+1}'}) + \sum_{s=t+K'}^{n-1} f_{\text{type}}(P_{s,i_s'}, P_{s+1,i_{s+1}'}). \qquad (2.17)$$

2.5.2 Estimating the Cost of Compactness

We estimate the cost of compactness based on regular polygons. The more edges a regular polygon has, the more compact it is. We assume that, at each step, we aggregate the two patches that are the least compact. Moreover, we assume that the shared boundary of the two patches has the least number of edges. We use N_{ext} to denote the edge number of the region's exterior boundaries. As the exterior boundaries will not be changed by aggregation, N_{ext} is a constant. Note that the boundary between two patches is not necessarily connected; for example, see the dark boundary with three edges in Figure 2.11a. For subdivision $P_{t,i}$, we denote by $B(P_{t,i})$ the set of interior boundaries and denote by $b_{\text{min}}(P_{t,i})$ the boundary with the smallest number of edges. For our estimation, the set of interior boundaries at time $t+1$ is $B(P_{t+1,i_{t+1}''}) = B(P_{t,i}) - \{b_{\text{min}}(P_{t,i})\}$. The estimated number of the edges for such a subdivision, $P_{t+1,i_{t+1}''}$, is

$$N_{t+1,i_{t+1}''} = N_{\text{ext}} + \sum_{b \in B(P_{t+1,i_{t+1}''})} \|b\|, \qquad (2.18)$$

where notation $\|b\|$ represents the number of boundary b's edges.

From subdivision $P_{t,i}$ to subdivision $P_{t+1,i_{t+1}''}$, we get a new patch because of the aggregation. The new patch is certainly less compact than a regular polygon with $N_{t+1,i_{t+1}''}$ edges. In order to estimate the compactness of the new patch, we assume that the new patch has the shape of a regular polygon with $N_{t+1,i_{t+1}''}$ edges (see Equation 2.18). A regular polygon with N edges has compactness

$$c_{\text{reg}}(N) = \sqrt{\frac{\pi}{N} / \tan\frac{\pi}{N}}.$$

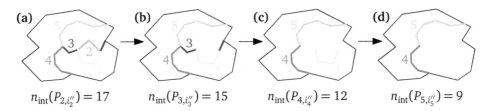

$$n_{\text{int}}(P_{2,i_2''}) = 17 \qquad n_{\text{int}}(P_{3,i_3''}) = 15 \qquad n_{\text{int}}(P_{4,i_4''}) = 12 \qquad n_{\text{int}}(P_{5,i_5''}) = 9$$

Figure 2.11: An "aggregation sequence" for computing the estimated cost of compactness h_{comp} (see Equations 2.19 and 2.20), based on the number of edges. At each step we remove the boundary with the fewest edges. The numbers represent the numbers of the interior boundaries' edges. Note that this aggregation sequence is impossible in reality, but it is fine for estimating (see the argument in Section 2.5.1). This example corresponds to the aggregation step in Figure 2.7b.

Note that compactness $c_{\text{reg}}(\mathcal{N})$ increases with increasing $\mathcal{N}$. A patch with $\mathcal{N}_{t+1,i_{t+1}''}$ edges has compactness $c_{\text{reg}}(\mathcal{N}_{t+1,i_{t+1}''})$. According to our previous assumption, at each step we are always able to aggregate the two patches that are the least compact in the subdivision. We denote the compactness values of the two patches by $c_{\text{min1}}(P_{t,i})$ and $c_{\text{min2}}(P_{t,i})$. Recall that we use $C(P_{t,i})$ to denote the set of compactness values of the patches in subdivision $P_{t,i}$ (see Section 2.2.2). Then the set of compactness values for subdivision $P_{t+1,i_{t+1}''}$ is

$$C(P_{t+1,i_{t+1}''}) = C(P_{s,i}) \cup \{c_{\text{reg}}(\mathcal{N}_{t+1,i_{t+1}''})\} \setminus \{c_{\text{min1}}(P_{t,i}), c_{\text{min2}}(P_{t,i})\}.$$

We compute the estimated average compactness by calculating the average of the values in set $C(P_{t+1,i_{t+1}''})$. Finally, we compute the estimated cost of compactness for subdivision $P_{t+1,i_{t+1}''}$ by Equation 2.4.

For subdivision $P_{t,i}$, let $(P_{t,i} = P_{t,i''}, P_{t+1,i_{t+1}''}, \ldots, P_{n,i_n''} = P_{\text{goal}})$ be the path that always removes the two smallest compactnesses and gains a compactness of the constructed regular polygon. The estimated cost of compactness is

$$h_{\text{comp}}(P_{t,i}) = \sum_{s=t}^{n-1} f_{\text{comp}}(P_{s,i_s''}). \tag{2.19}$$

When overestimating, we assume that each patch in the subdivision is extremely noncompact, that is, each patch has compactness 0. One may ask if this assumption is too much. It is indeed too much for one subdivision, but it is just fine for the whole sequence as we overestimate for only a certain number of subdivisions. Based on the assumption, the cost of compactness is $f_{\text{comp}}(P_{s,i''}) = 1/(n-2)$, according to Equation 2.4. When we need to overestimate K' steps (see Equation 2.15), we revise the estimated cost of compactness to

$$h_{\text{comp}}(P_{t,i}) = \sum_{s=t}^{t+K'-1} \frac{1}{n-2} + \sum_{s=t+K'}^{n-1} f_{\text{comp}}(P_{s,i_s''}). \tag{2.20}$$

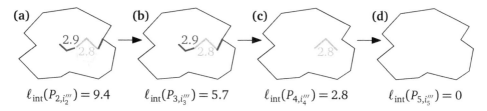

(a)   **(b)**   **(c)**   **(d)**

$\ell_{\text{int}}(P_{2,i_2'''}) = 9.4$ $\ell_{\text{int}}(P_{3,i_3'''}) = 5.7$ $\ell_{\text{int}}(P_{4,i_4'''}) = 2.8$ $\ell_{\text{int}}(P_{5,i_5'''}) = 0$

Figure 2.12: An "aggregation sequence" for computing the estimated cost of length h_{lgth} (see Equations 2.21 and 2.22), based on the lengths of interior boundaries. At each step, we keep the necessary number of interior boundaries with least lengths in order to find a lower bound of the total length of the interior boundaries, i.e., $\ell_{\text{int}}(P_{s,i'''})$. The numbers represent the lengths of the interior boundaries. Note that this aggregation sequence is impossible in reality, but it is fine for estimating (see the argument in Section 2.5.1). This example corresponds to the aggregation step in Figure 2.7b.

2.5.3 Estimating the Cost of Length

At time s, there are $n-s+1$ patches. There can be as few as $n-s$ interior boundaries. In order to find a lower bound for the cost of length, we keep only the necessary number, $n-s$, of shortest boundaries at each step (see Figure 2.12). Then, we compute the estimated cost of length according to Equation 2.6.

For subdivision $P_{t,i}$, let $(P_{t,i} = P_{t,i_t'''}, P_{t+1,i_{t+1}'''}, \dots, P_{n,i_n'''} = P_{\text{goal}})$ be the path that always keeps the necessary number of shortest interior boundaries. The estimated cost of length is

$$h_{\text{lgth}}(P_{t,i}) = \sum_{s=t}^{n-1} f_{\text{lgth}}(P_{s,i_s'''}). \tag{2.21}$$

When overestimating, we use the interior length of subdivision $P_{t,i}$ as the cost of length for each of the first K' steps (see Equation 2.15), even though we are removing interior boundaries step by step. As a result, we revise Formula 2.21 to

$$h_{\text{lgth}}(P_{t,i}) = \sum_{s=t}^{t+K'-1} f_{\text{lgth}}(P_{t,i}) + \sum_{s=t+K'}^{n-1} f_{\text{lgth}}(P_{s,i_s'''}). \tag{2.22}$$

2.5.4 Combining Estimated Costs

In accordance with our two combinatorial costs in Section 2.2.4, we define two estimated-cost functions:

$$h_1(P_{t,i}) = (1-\lambda)h_{\text{type}}(P_{t,i}) + \lambda h_{\text{comp}}(P_{t,i}), \tag{2.23}$$

and

$$h_2(P_{t,i}) = (1-\lambda)h_{\text{type}}(P_{t,i}) + \lambda h_{\text{lgth}}(P_{t,i}). \tag{2.24}$$

2.6   Integer Linear Programming

Linear programming is a method to optimize a *linear objective* subject to a set of *linear constraints* with some *variables*. Suppose that we are selling coffee. We have 3.5 kg of coffee powder and 10 kg of water. We mix the powder and the water to provide two kinds coffee with different intensities in terms of mass: 40% and 20%. The profits of them are respectively 5€ and 4€. Our aim is to maximize the total profit of selling coffee. If we offer x kg and y kg of the two kinds of coffee, then x and y are our variables. Our objective is to

$$\text{maximize} \quad 5x + 4y.$$

To provide x kg of coffee with intensity 40%, we need to use $0.4x$ kg of coffee powder and $0.6x$ kg of water. Analogously, we need $0.2y$ kg of powder and $0.8y$ kg of water to produce y kg of coffee with intensity 20%. As a result, we have four constraints:

$$0.4x + 0.2y \leq 3.5,$$
$$0.6x + 0.8y \leq 10, \text{ and}$$
$$x, y \geq 0.$$

With the objective and the constraints, we have set up a *linear program* (LP). We observed that all the feasible solutions, i.e., pairs of (x, y), fall in the gray area of Figure 2.13a. Drawing a line with slope $-\frac{5}{4}$, we see that every pair of (x, y) lying on the line yields the same result for $5x + 4y$, the profit we want to maximize. For example, every pair of (x, y) lying on the dashed line in Figure 2.13a yields profit 40€. If we move the dashed line to the upper right, then we are able to achieve a larger value for $5x + 4y$. In order to maximize the profit, we move the dashed line to the upper right as much as possible and, at the same time, make sure that it still intersects with the gray area. Note that if the dashed line does not intersect with the gray area, then there is no feasible pair of (x, y) on the dashed line anymore. As a result, we get the optimal solution when the dashed line hits point A, where the profit is $5 \cdot 4 + 4 \cdot 9.5 = 58$€. Karmarkar [Kar84] proved that an LP can be solved in polynomial time.

Now we change our problem a bit. We wish to sell coffee in jugs, where each jug contains exactly 1 kg of coffee with intensity 40% or 20%. Our question becomes how many jugs of each kind of coffee we should sell in order to maximize the profit. If we sell the two kinds of coffee respectively x' and y' jugs, then the problem becomes:

$$\begin{aligned}
\text{maximize} \quad & 5x' + 4y' \\
\text{subject to} \quad & 0.4x' + 0.2y' \leq 3.5, \\
& 0.6x' + 0.8y' \leq 10, \\
& x', y' \geq 0, \\
\text{and} \quad & x', y' \in \mathbb{Z}.
\end{aligned}$$

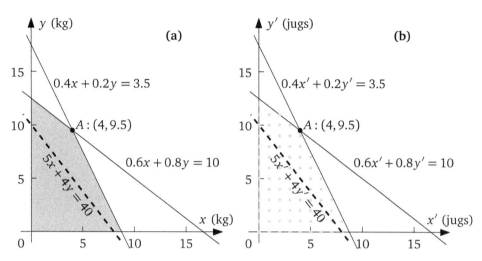

Figure 2.13: Examples of linear programming (a) and integer linear programming (b). In (a), any point in the gray area is a feasible solution; in (b), only the gray points are feasible solutions.

For this problem, only the pairs of (x', y') represented by the gray dots of Figure 2.13b are feasible solutions (point A is no longer a feasible solution in this case). In order to maximize our profit, we should move the dashed line to the upper right as much as possible and, at the same time, make sure that it hits at least one of the gray dots. To solve such a problem is known as *integer linear programming*, which is NP-complete. Despite the fact, there are mathematical solvers yielding optimal solutions for some NP-complete problems in reasonable time [HW17]. By using these solvers, we benefit from every improvement, by their producers, for the same class of problems [HW17]. The general form of an *integer linear program* (ILP) is

$$\text{maximize} \quad C^{\mathsf{T}} X$$
$$\text{subject to} \quad E X \leq H,$$
$$X \geq 0,$$
$$\text{and} \quad X \in \mathbb{Z}^I,$$

where vector X represents integer variables, vector $C \in \mathbb{R}^I$, vector $H \in \mathbb{R}^J$, and E is a $(J \times I)$-matrix over the reals. Furthermore, if we require

$$X \in \{0, 1\}^I,$$

then we have only binary variables for an ILP. Binary variables are important because they occur regularly in optimizations [BHM77, Section 9.2]. Also, an ILP with general (bounded) integer variables can always be translated to an ILP with binary variables [Wil09, Section 2.3]. We are going to use binary variables in our ILP because it is more intuitive to model our problem using binary variables than using other integers.

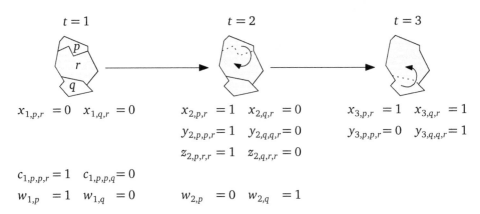

$$x_{1,p,r} = 0 \quad x_{1,q,r} = 0$$

$$x_{2,p,r} = 1 \quad x_{2,q,r} = 0$$
$$y_{2,p,p,r} = 1 \quad y_{2,q,q,r} = 0$$
$$z_{2,p,r,r} = 1 \quad z_{2,q,r,r} = 0$$

$$x_{3,p,r} = 1 \quad x_{3,q,r} = 1$$
$$y_{3,p,p,r} = 0 \quad y_{3,q,q,r} = 1$$

$$c_{1,p,p,r} = 1 \quad c_{1,p,p,q} = 0$$
$$w_{1,p} = 1 \quad w_{1,q} = 0$$

$$w_{2,p} = 0 \quad w_{2,q} = 1$$

Figure 2.14: Some examples of the five sets of variables for our ILP, x, y, z, c, and w. The arrows with curly arms show the aggregation steps, and the dotted lines represent the removed boundaries by the aggregation steps. There are some blank spaces in the rows of the variables because there is no corresponding variable at the specific times.

We want to compare the A* algorithm with integer linear programming in finding optimal sequences for our aggregation problem. Since integer linear programming can handle only linear constraints, we define the compactness of a subdivision as the length of the subdivision's interior boundaries. That is, we use cost function g_2 (see Equation 2.10). Our basic idea is to formalize the problem of finding a shortest path as an ILP. Then we solve this ILP by minimizing the total cost. We define the *center* of a patch as the polygon to which other polygons in the same patch are assigned. At the beginning, every patch consists of only one polygon, and this polygon is the center of the patch. When we aggregate patch u into patch v, all the polygons of u are assigned to the center of v, and the type of u's polygons are changed to the type of v's center. In the following, we show how to formalize our problem as an ILP. For simplicity, we sometimes denote by *patch r* the patch using polygon r as the center at time t.

2.6.1 Variables

Our problem is to decide centers for polygons to be assigned. Each question of type "Is polygon p assigned to center r?" can be answered with "yes" or "no". Hence, we use binary (0–1) variables. We need five sets of variables in order to formulate our pathfinding problem as an ILP. Recall that We use $T = \{1, 2, \ldots, n\}$ to represent the set of times and use P to denote the set of n polygons on the start map (see Section 2.1). The first set of variables is used to tell the program our rules for area aggregation. We introduce the variable

$$x_{t,p,r} \in \{0, 1\} \qquad \forall t \in T, \forall p, r \in P$$

with the intended meaning $x_{t,p,r} = 1$ if and only if polygon p is assigned to polygon r at time t (see Figure 2.14 for some examples). If a polygon is a center at time t, then the polygon must be assigned to itself, that is, $x_{t,r,r} = 1$.

We use the second set of variables in order to compute the cost of type change. We introduce

$$y_{t,p,o,r} \in \{0,1\} \qquad \forall t \in T \setminus \{1\}, \forall p, o, r \in P$$

with the intended meaning $y_{t,p,o,r} = 1$ if and only if polygon p is assigned to center o at time $t - 1$ and assigned to center r at time t (see Figure 2.14). Specifically, case $y_{t,p,o,o} = 1$ means that polygon p is assigned to the same center at times $t - 1$ and t.

We need a third set of variables for computing the cost of length. We introduce

$$z_{t,p,q,r} \in \{0,1\} \qquad \forall t \in T \setminus \{1,n\}, \forall p, q, r \in P$$

with the intended meaning $z_{t,p,q,r} = 1$ if and only if polygons p and q are both assigned to center r at time t (p and q are in the same patch). In this case, their common boundary should be removed (see Figure 2.14). When variable $z_{t,p,q,r} = 1$ and $p = q$, we define the length of their common boundary to be 0 because we shall not remove any. Note that time $t \in T \setminus \{1,n\}$. We do not need $z_{t,p,q,r}$ for time $t = 1$ because there are no two polygons in the same patch. Namely, it always holds $z_{1,p,q,r} = 0$, which does not help in our ILP. We do not need $z_{t,p,q,r}$ for time $t = n$ because all the polygons will be in the same patch. In this case, Equation $z_{n,p,q,r} = 1$ always holds, which does not help in our ILP, either.

We use a fourth set of variables to guarantee contiguity of each patch. In other words, we aggregate two patches only when they are neighbors (adjacent). We introduce

$$c_{t,p,o,r} \in \{0,1\} \qquad \forall t \in T \setminus \{n-1,n\}, \forall p, o, r \in P \text{ with } o \neq r,$$

with the intended meaning $c_{t,p,o,r} = 1$ if and only if, at time t, polygon p is assigned to center o, and p has a neighbor assigned to center r (see Figures 2.14 and 2.15 for examples). We do not need variable $c_{t,p,o,r}$ for time $t = n-1$ because there are only two patches left, and they must be neighbors.

Our last set of variables is needed to enforce that every aggregation step involves a smallest patch. We define

$$w_{t,o} \in \{0,1\} \qquad \forall t \in T \setminus \{n\}, \forall o \in P$$

with $w_{t,o} = 1$ meaning if and only if, at time t, patch o is the smallest patch that is involved in the aggregation step from time t to time $t - 1$ (see for example Figure 2.14).

In total, the number of variables in our ILP formulation is $O(n^4)$.

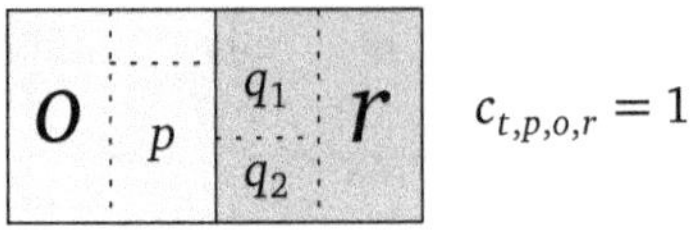

Figure 2.15: There are two patches, which respectively use polygons o and r as their centers. Polygons in the same patch are separated by dotted lines. Polygon p, in patch o, has two neighbors assigned to center r, i.e., polygons q_1 and q_2. In this case, patches o and r are neighbors and can be aggregated.

2.6.2 Objective

We want to minimize a weighted sum of the two costs, the cost of type change and the cost of length (analogous to Equation 2.10). That is, our objective is to

$$\text{minimize} \quad (1-\lambda)F_{\text{type}} + \lambda F_{\text{lgth}},$$

where λ, as in Equation 2.10, is a parameter to assign importances of F_{type} and F_{lgth}. According to the cost introduced in Section 2.2.1, we compute the total cost of type change by

$$F_{\text{type}} = \sum_{t=2}^{n}\sum_{p\in P}\sum_{o\in P}\sum_{r\in P}\left(\frac{a_p}{A_R}\cdot\frac{d_{\text{type}}(T(o),T(r))}{d_{\text{type\_max}}}\cdot y_{t,p,o,r}\right),$$

where, similar to Equation 2.1, a_p is the area of polygon p, A_R is the area of the region, and $T(o)$ and $T(r)$ are the types of centers (polygons) o and r.

We also wish to minimize the overall interior lengths of all the intermediate subdivisions. As discussed in Section 2.2.3, we use the length of the interior boundaries as an alternative to compactness. Recall that $B(P_{\text{start}})$ is the set of interior boundaries at time $t = 1$ (see Section 2.2.3). We sum up the normalized lengths of the remaining interior boundaries of all the intermediate subdivisions by

$$F_{\text{lgth}} = \frac{1}{n-2}\sum_{t=2}^{n-1}\frac{\sum_{b\in B(P_{\text{start}})}|b| - \frac{1}{2}\sum_{p\in P}\sum_{q\in P}\sum_{r\in P}\left(|b_{pq}|\cdot z_{t,p,q,r}\right)}{D(t)}, \qquad (2.25)$$

where variable b_{pq} represents the common boundary between polygons p and q. We define the length of the common boundary to be 0 (i.e., $|b_{pq}| = 0$) if $p = q$ because there is no boundary to be removed in this case. Function $D(t)$, defined by Equation 2.7, is used to normalize the cost of length. As in Equation 2.6, we use denominator $n-2$ to balance between the cost of type change and the cost of length. Integrating Equation 2.7 into Equation 2.25, we have

$$F_{\text{lgth}} = \frac{n-1}{n-2}\sum_{t=2}^{n-1}\left(\frac{1}{n-t} - \frac{\sum_{p\in P}\sum_{q\in P}\sum_{r\in P}\left(|b_{pq}|\cdot z_{t,p,q,r}\right)}{2(n-t)\sum_{b\in B(P_{\text{start}})}|b|}\right).$$

2.6.3 Constraints

In order to formulate our aggregation problem as an ILP, we restrict the variables introduced in Section 2.6.1 by setting up constraints. Recall that the intended meaning of $x_{t,p,r} = 1$ is if and only if polygon p is assigned to center r at time t. To realize this functionality, our first constraint is that polygon p is assigned to exactly one center at time t. To this end, we require that

$$\sum_{r \in P} x_{t,p,r} = 1 \qquad\qquad \forall t \in T, \forall p \in P. \qquad\qquad (2.26)$$

The next constraint is that polygon r is available to be assigned by other polygons only when r is a center. In our case, if polygon r is a center, then it must be assigned to itself, that is, $x_{t,r,r} = 1$. If r is not a center, we have variable $x_{t,r,r} = 0$. In either case, we have

$$x_{t,p,r} \leq x_{t,r,r} \qquad\qquad \forall t \in T, \forall p, r \in P. \qquad\qquad (2.27)$$

Aggregating a patch into another one results in the number of centers decreasing by 1. We achieve that exactly one patch is aggregated into another by specifying the number of centers for each point in time, that is,

$$\sum_{r \in P} x_{t,r,r} = n - t + 1 \qquad\qquad \forall t \in T, \qquad\qquad (2.28)$$

where polygon r is a center at time t if and only if $x_{t,r,r} = 1$.

When a patch is aggregated into another one, the center of the former will not be used as a center anymore. Hence, we have

$$x_{t,r,r} \leq x_{t-1,r,r} \qquad\qquad \forall t \in T \setminus \{1\}, \forall r \in P. \qquad\qquad (2.29)$$

On the start map, there are some polygons with the goal type, T_{goal} (see definition in Section 2.5.1). At time $t = n$, all polygons are aggregated into one patch. This patch must have type T_{goal}. In other words, the center of this patch must be one of the polygons with type T_{goal} on the start map:

$$\sum_{r \in P:\, T(r)=T_{goal}} x_{n,r,r} = 1, \qquad\qquad (2.30)$$

where $T(r)$ is the type of polygon r at time $t = 1$.

Next, we restrict binary variable $y_{t,p,o,r}$, introduced in Section 2.6.1. Recall that the intended meaning of $y_{t,p,o,r} = 1$ is if and only if polygon p is assigned to center o at time $t-1$ and to center r at time t. To enforce this, we use two types of constraints.

First, if polygon p is assigned to center o at time $t-1$ ($x_{t-1,p,o} = 1$) and assigned to center r at time t ($x_{t,p,r} = 1$), we have variable $y_{t,p,o,r} = 1$. This requirement is expressed by

$$y_{t,p,o,r} \geq x_{t-1,p,o} + x_{t,p,r} - 1 \qquad \forall t \in T \setminus \{1\}, \forall p, o, r \in P. \qquad\qquad (2.31)$$

Second, if p is not assigned to o at $t-1$ ($x_{t-1,p,o} = 0$) and/or p is not assigned to r at time t ($x_{t,p,o} = 0$), we have variable $y_{t,p,o,r} = 0$. This requirement is expressed by

$$\left. \begin{aligned} y_{t,p,o,r} &\leq x_{t-1,p,o} \\ y_{t,p,o,r} &\leq x_{t,p,r} \end{aligned} \right\} \qquad \forall t \in T \setminus \{1\}, \forall p, o, r \in P. \tag{2.32}$$

In Section 2.6.1, we introduced binary variable $z_{t,p,q,r}$. Recall that the intended meaning of $z_{t,p,q,r} = 1$ is if and only if polygons p and q are both in patch r at time t. To enforce this, we need three types of constraints.

First, if two polygons p and q are assigned to center r at time t ($x_{t,p,r} = 1$ and $x_{t,q,r} = 1$), we have variable $z_{t,p,q,r} = 1$. This requirement is expressed by

$$z_{t,p,q,r} \geq x_{t,p,r} + x_{t,q,r} - 1 \qquad \forall t \in T \setminus \{1, n\}, \forall p, q, r \in P. \tag{2.33}$$

Second, at time t, if p is not assigned to r ($x_{t,p,r} = 0$) and/or q is not assigned to r ($x_{t,q,r} = 0$), we have variable $z_{t,p,q,r} = 0$. This requirement is expressed by

$$\left. \begin{aligned} z_{t,p,q,r} &\leq x_{t,p,r} \\ z_{t,p,q,r} &\leq x_{t,q,r} \end{aligned} \right\} \qquad \forall t \in T \setminus \{1, n\}, \forall p, q, r \in P. \tag{2.34}$$

Third, we introduce an abbreviation that will be helpful to express the last type of constraint involving variable $z_{t,p,q,r}$:

$$z_{t,p,q} = \sum_{r \in P} z_{t,p,q,r} \qquad \forall t \in T \setminus \{1, n\}, \forall p, q \in P, \tag{2.35}$$

where the reason we do not need $z_{t,p,q}$ for $t = 1$ or $t = n$ is the same as for $z_{t,p,q,r}$ (see Section 2.6.1). Variable $z_{t,p,q}$ expresses whether, at time t, polygons p and q are in the same patch ($z_{t,p,q} = 1$) or not ($z_{t,p,q} = 0$). Note that constraints (2.26) and (2.34) ensure that polygons p and q can be assigned to one common center at most; therefore, we have $z_{t,p,q} \leq 1$. We use our new variable $z_{t,p,q}$ to express the following requirement: If two polygons have been aggregated into one patch, they will always be in the same patch at later times—although the center of their common patch may change. In other words, variable $z_{t,p,q}$ is monotonically increasing as a function of time t:

$$z_{t,p,q} \geq z_{t-1,p,q} \qquad \forall t \in \{3, 4, \ldots, n-1\}, \forall p, q \in P. \tag{2.36}$$

Now we present our constraints of ensuring contiguity inside a patch. This problem has received considerable attention in integer linear programming. Usually, a subdivision is represented by a graph (see Figure 2.5). Zoltners and Sinha [ZS83] regarded each node as a center. For each center, they found a shortest path to each of the other nodes. Then, they required that a center can be assigned by a node only if at least one immediate predecessor of the node in the shortest path had been assigned to the center. Although this requirement makes their problem easier to be solved, it excludes many feasible patches. Williams [Wil02] built an optimal spanning tree for the nodes. In order to ensure contiguity, the method picks a user-specified number of nodes that constitute an optimal subtree of the previously built spanning tree. For a given center, Cova and Church [CC00] were able to find all the contiguous patches. In their method, when a node is to be assigned to a center, a path from the node to the center was demanded that each node of the path is assigned to the center. Similarly, Shirabe [Shi05] modeled the contiguity problem as a network flow. He required that there must be a path so that some fluid can flow from a node to a sink (center). Oehrlein and Haunert [OH17] utilized a method based on *vertex separators*. Given center r and node p, a separator is a set of nodes such that any path from r to p will contain at least one node of the set. The contiguity between center r and node p is ensured if each of the separators contains at least one node assigned to the center. The last four ideas can be adapted into our method as we do not wish to exclude any possible solutions. However, we use an idea that is more intuitive for our problem since we aggregate step by step.

We aggregate two patches only if they are neighbors. To ensure this, we need binary variable $c_{t,p,o,r}$ introduced in Section 2.6.1. Recall that the intended meaning of $c_{t,p,o,r} = 1$ is if and only if, at time t, polygon p of patch o has at least one neighboring polygon in patch r. To enforce this behavior of $c_{t,p,o,r}$, we need four types of constraints.

First, polygon p must actually be assigned to center o at time t ($x_{t,p,o} = 1$). In contrast, if p is not assigned to o ($x_{t,p,o} = 0$), then variable $c_{t,p,o,r}$ is impossible to tell if patch o and patch r are neighbors. In this case, we must not aggregate the two patches ($c_{t,p,o,r} = 0$); otherwise, we may end up having noncontiguous patches. As a result,

$$c_{t,p,o,r} \leq x_{t,p,o} \qquad \begin{aligned} &\forall t \in T \setminus \{n-1, n\}, \\ &\forall p, o, r \in P \text{ with } o \neq r. \end{aligned} \qquad (2.37)$$

Second, at time t, at least one of polygon p's neighbor(s), say, polygon q has to be assigned to center r ($x_{t,q,r} = 1$). If not, then variable $c_{t,p,o,r}$ is impossible to tell if patches o and r are neighbors. Analogous to the condition of constraint (2.37), we have

$$c_{t,p,o,r} \leq \sum_{q \in N_{\text{nbr}}(p)} x_{t,q,r} \qquad \begin{aligned} &\forall t \in T \setminus \{n-1, n\}, \\ &\forall p, o, r \in P \text{ with } o \neq r, \end{aligned} \qquad (2.38)$$

where $N_{\text{nbr}}(p)$ represents the set of polygons adjacent to p.

Third, if polygon p is in patch o ($x_{t,p,o} = 1$) and p has at least one neighbor, say, polygon q in patch r ($x_{t,q,r} = 1$), then we must enforce variable $c_{t,p,o,r} = 1$ (according to the definition of this variable). We have

$$c_{t,p,o,r} \geq x_{t,p,o} + x_{t,q,r} - 1 \qquad \begin{aligned} &\forall t \in T \setminus \{n-1, n\}, \\ &\forall p, o, r \in P \text{ with } o \neq r, \forall q \in N_{\text{nbr}}(p). \end{aligned} \qquad (2.39)$$

Fourth, if we aggregate patch o into patch r from time $t-1$ to time t, we have variable $y_{t,o,o,r} = 1$ (see the definition of this variable in Section 2.6.1). In this case, we must make sure that the two patches are actually neighbors at time $t-1$. That is to say, at least one of patch o's polygons has at least one neighbor in patch r at time $t-1$. If not, we have $y_{t,o,o,r} = 0$. That is, it holds

$$y_{t,o,o,r} \le \sum_{p \in P} c_{t-1,p,o,r} \qquad\qquad \forall t \in T \setminus \{1,n\}, \forall o, r \in P \text{ with } o \ne r. \qquad (2.40)$$

If we do not require that each aggregation step must involve a smallest patch, then we only need constraints (2.26)–(2.40) and variables $x_{t,p,r}$, $y_{t,p,o,r}$, $z_{t,p,q,r}$, and $c_{t,p,o,r}$. If we insist on involving a smallest patch at each step, then we need more variables and more constraints.

Aggregation involving a smallest patch

In order to make sure that each of our aggregation steps involves a smallest patch, we need another type of variable, $w_{t,o}$. Recall that the intended meaning of $w_{t,o} = 1$ is if and only if polygon o is the center of a smallest patch at time t. We will use this to enforce that this patch is involved in the aggregation step from time t to $t+1$. At any time t, we pick exactly one smallest patch (there can be many) and aggregate it with one of its neighbors; we do not care whether or not the neighbor is a smallest one. Therefore, we have

$$\sum_{o \in P} w_{t,o} = 1 \qquad\qquad \forall t \in T \setminus \{n\}. \qquad (2.41)$$

Assume that patch o is the smallest patch involved in the aggregation step from t to $t+1$ and that we are aggregating patch o and another patch, say, r. There can be two cases. We aggregate o into r or aggregate r into o. In the first case, we have variable $y_{t+1,o,o,r} = 1$, and, in the second case, we have $y_{t+1,r,r,o} = 1$. Either of the two cases implies that polygon o is indeed a center at time t, that is, $x_{t,o,o} = 1$. In order to enforce that the aggregation step involves patch o and another patch, we must make sure $y_{t+1,o,o,r} = 1$ or $y_{t+1,r,r,o} = 1$ when $w_{t,o} = 1$. Consequently, we use the constraint

$$w_{t,o} \le \sum_{r \in P \setminus \{o\}} \left(y_{t+1,o,o,r} + y_{t+1,r,r,o} \right) \qquad \forall t \in T \setminus \{n\}, \forall o \in P. \qquad (2.42)$$

Now we need to make sure that patch o with $w_{t,o} = 1$ is indeed a smallest patch at time t. We define variable $A_{t,r}$ as the area of patch r at time t. That is, we have

$$A_{t,r} = \sum_{p \in P} a_p \cdot x_{t,p,r},$$

where a_p is the area of polygon p and, as viewed by the ILP, is a constant. Area $A_{t,r}$ is positive if and only if polygon r is a center at time t $(x_{t,r,r} = 1)$. We define constant M as a very large number to help us construct the corresponding constraints. It suffices to set M to the area of the whole region, i.e., $M = A_R$ (see Equation 2.1). We require

$$A_{t,o} - M(1 - w_{t,o}) \leq A_{t,r} + M(1 - x_{t,r,r}) \qquad \begin{array}{l} \forall t \in T \setminus \{n\}, \\ \forall o, r \in P \text{ with } o \neq r. \end{array} \qquad (2.43)$$

This constraint takes effect only when $w_{t,o} = 1$ and $x_{t,r,r} = 1$, which indicates that patch o is smaller than or equal to all the other existing patches at time t.

In order to compute an aggregation sequence involving a smallest patch at each step, we need all the five types of variables and all the constraints (2.26)–(2.43). In total, the number of constraints is $O(n^4)$.

2.7 Case Study

We have implemented our methods based on C# (Microsoft Visual Studio 2017) and ArcObjects SDK 10.6.0. We used the IBM ILOG CPLEX Optimization Studio 12.6.3.0 to solve our ILP. Our prototype is open access on GitHub[1]. We ran our case study under 64-bit Windows 10 on Intel(R) Core(TM) i7-6700 CPU @ 3.40 GHz with 4 cores; the computer has 16 GB RAM. We measured processing time by the built-in C# class *Stopwatch*. As required by ArcObjects SDK 10.6.0, we specified our program to run on the 32-bit platform. We added a post-build task about "largeaddressaware" in Microsoft Visual Studio so that we were able to use up to 3 GB of the main memory[2]. Our CPLEX version may declare an optimal solution while it is not really optimal. To fix this problem, we had to disable both primal and dual presolve reductions[3].

We tested our method on a dataset from the German topographic database ATKIS DLM 50. The dataset represents the place "Buchholz in der Nordheide" at scale 1 : 50,000. Our start map is the result of collapsing areas by Haunert [Hau09, Chapter 6]. The start map has 5,537 polygons. Our goal map was generalized from the start map by Haunert and Wolff [HW10a], setting the scale to 1 : 250,000 (see Figure 2.16). The goal map has 734 polygons, which means that there are $N = 734$ regions. The distribution of region sizes is shown in Figure 2.17. We used a tree-based method introduced by Rada et al. [Rad+89] to define the distances of the types; the distance is the "number of edges" that we need to travel from one node to another node in the tree of type hierarchy[4] (see Figure 2.18). For example, the dis-

---

[1]   https://github.com/IGNF/ContinuousGeneralisation, Accessed: Jun 18, 2018.
[2]   The details of the setting can be found at http://stackoverflow.com/questions/2597790/can-i-set-largeaddressaware-from-within-visual-studio, Accessed: Nov 1, 2017.
[3]   For more details about the problem, see http://www-01.ibm.com/support/docview.wss?uid=swg1RS02094, Accessed: Nov 12, 2017.
[4]   More information about land-cover types can be found at http://www.atkis.de/dstinfo/dstinfo2.dst_gliederung, Accessed: Nov 1, 2017.

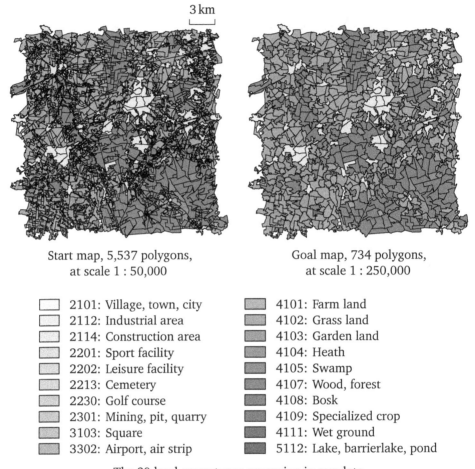

Start map, 5,537 polygons,   Goal map, 734 polygons,
at scale 1 : 50,000   at scale 1 : 250,000

☐ 2101: Village, town, city		☐ 4101: Farm land
☐ 2112: Industrial area		☐ 4102: Grass land
☐ 2114: Construction area		☐ 4103: Garden land
☐ 2201: Sport facility		☐ 4104: Heath
☐ 2202: Leisure facility		☐ 4105: Swamp
☐ 2213: Cemetery		☐ 4107: Wood, forest
☐ 2230: Golf course		☐ 4108: Bosk
☐ 2301: Mining, pit, quarry		☐ 4109: Specialized crop
☐ 3103: Square		☐ 4111: Wet ground
☐ 3302: Airport, air strip		☐ 5112: Lake, barrierlake, pond

The 20 land-cover types appearing in our data

Figure 2.16: The data of our case study.

tance from type *village* to type *fence* is 2, to type *street* is 4, and to type *farm land* is 6.
In this tree, the maximum distance is 6, which means $d_{\text{type\_max}} = 6$ for Equation 2.1.
According to Rada et al. [Rad+89], the resulting cost function for type change is a
metric.

2.7.1 Using Costs of Type Change and Compactness

As illustrated in Section 2.2.4, we compare the A* algorithm and the greedy algorithm using $g_1(P_{t,i})$, which is a combination of the costs of type change and compactness (see Equation 2.9). For A*, we overestimated whenever we could not find
a solution after having visited W nodes (see Section 2.5). We tried $W = 200,000$

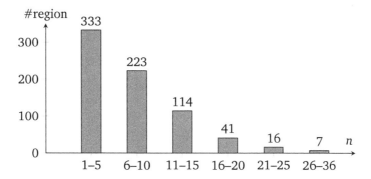

Figure 2.17: Distribution of the region sizes: the y-axis shows how many regions of a given size range are contained in our dataset.

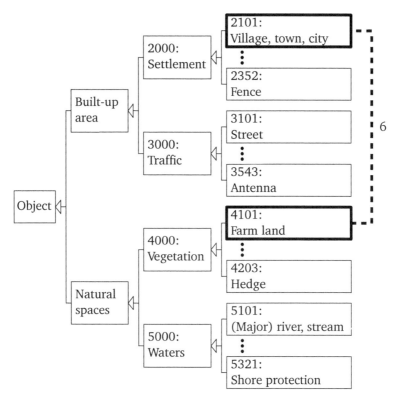

Figure 2.18: The tree of type hierarchy used in our case study. For example, the distance between types *village* and *farm land* is 6.

and $W = 400{,}000$ (if we could use more main memory, then we could test by using some larger W). The results are shown in Table 2.1. Comparing to A*, the greedy algorithm visited fewer nodes and arcs in graph G_S and used much less time. However,

Table 2.1: A comparison of the greedy algorithm and A* when using cost function g_1 (see Equation 2.9). For A*, we used two settings, i.e., $W = 200{,}000$ and $W = 400{,}000$. Column #OS shows the numbers of regions that we obtained optimal solutions. Column #FS presents the numbers and the percentages of regions (out of $N = 734$) that we obtained feasible (non-optimal) solutions. Variable k_{sum} is the total number of repetitions. Columns #nodes and #arcs are the total numbers of nodes and arcs that A* visited (for instances where we needed overestimation, only the final attempt was counted). Columns $\sum g_{type}$, $\sum g_{comp}$, and $\sum g_1$ respectively denotes the sums of $g_{type}(P_{goal})$, $g_{comp}(P_{goal})$, and $g_1(P_{goal})$ over all the 734 instances (see Equations 2.2, 2.5, and 2.9). The percentage in the *Time* column is the fraction of the runtime spent on solving the instances that we obtained feasible solutions. For A*, the time needed for overestimation is included.

Methods	#OS	#FS	k_{sum}	#nodes	#arcs	$\sum g_{type}$	$\sum g_{comp}$	$\sum g_1$	Time (min)
Greedy	408	326 (44.4%)		$5.5\cdot10^3$	$4.8\cdot10^3$	53.2	188.2	120.7	0.1 (74.6%)
$A^*_{200,000}$	702	32 (4.4%)	102	$3.6\cdot10^6$	$5.7\cdot10^6$	51.4	183.2	117.3	51.6 (93.2%)
$A^*_{400,000}$	704	30 (4.1%)	89	$6.5\cdot10^6$	$9.8\cdot10^6$	51.4	183.1	117.2	93.1 (95.5%)

A* managed to find solutions with lower total cost, 117.3 (or 117.2), which is 2.8% less than the total cost of the greedy algorithm, 120.7. When $W = 200{,}000$, we are sure that we have found optimal solutions for 702 of the 734 regions (95.6%), while the greedy algorithm solved only 408 (55.6%) to optimality; see column #OS in Table 2.1. For the other 32 regions, both algorithms have found feasible solutions (see column #FS in Table 2.1). Although some of the feasible solutions may also be optimal, we cannot verify that only from the cost values.

In accordance with Section 2.5, for region with ID i we define k_i as the least number of repetitions that we do to find a feasible solution. We define the total number of repetitions as $k_{sum} = \sum_{i=1}^{N} k_i$, where $N = 734$ is the number of the regions. After increasing W to 400,000, A* found optimal aggregation sequences for only two more regions, but k_{sum} decreased quite a bit, from 102 to 89. The numbers of regions that needed certain overestimation steps are shown in Figure 2.19. Besides, A* visited more arcs and nodes, used more time, but got (slightly) less cost when increasing W to 400,000. Although the number of regions that needed overestimation is relatively small, A* spent most of the running time on those few regions: 4.4% and 4.1% of the regions caused 93.2% and 95.5% of the total running time, respectively (see Table 2.1).

The details of some regions are presented in Table 2.2. According to the entries with overestimation factor $K_i = 0$, we often have ratios $R_{type} = 1$ and $R_{comp} > 1$. When factor $K_i = 0$, we did not overestimate for region i. The estimated cost must be smaller or equal to the exact cost, which results in $R_{type} \geq 1$ and $R_{comp} \geq 1$. Ratio $R_{type} = 1$ means that our estimation for the cost of type change is the best. A larger R_{comp} means a poorer estimation for the cost of shape.

According to columns n and K of Table 2.2, $A^*_{200,000}$ managed to find optimal solutions for all the regions with fewer than 15 polygons, and only found feasible solutions for any region with more than 21 polygons. Among the 702 regions that $A^*_{200,000}$ solved to optimality, the greedy algorithm failed to find optimal solutions for 294 regions. Solutions of the greedy algorithm cost at most 41.7% more

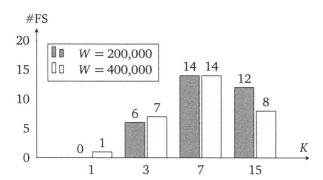

Figure 2.19: The numbers of regions where A* was forced to use the given overestimation parameters in order to find a solution without exploring more than $W \in \{200{,}000;\ 400{,}000\}$ nodes of the subdivision graph.

than solutions of $A^{*}_{200,000}$; for region 85, the greedy algorithm yields a solution of cost 0.777, while the solution of $A^{*}_{200,000}$ has cost 0.548 (see Figure 2.20). As the patches in the two sequences are the same, the two results have the same cost of compactness. The main difference is the choice of the first step, from 8 patches to 7. When aggregating the smallest patch on the start map with the surrounding patch, our greedy algorithm chooses the type which is closer to the goal type. In this case, the smallest patch has type 5112, and the surrounding one has 2112. The type of the goal patch is 4102. According to Figure 2.18, type distances $d_{type}(5112, 4102) = 4$ and $d_{type}(2112, 4102) = 6$. As a result, our greedy algorithm uses 5112 as the type for the new patch. This choice is a big mistake because the type of the largest patch on the start map will have to be changed twice during the aggregation. These changes cause a cost more than the sequence obtained by $A^{*}_{200,000}$, where the largest patch on the start map is changed to the target type directly.

Among the 32 regions that $A^{*}_{200,000}$ failed to solve optimally, the greedy algorithm outperformed $A^{*}_{200,000}$ for 15 regions (46.9%). Among these, solutions of the greedy algorithm cost at most 15.9% less than solutions of $A^{*}_{200,000}$; for region 543, the greedy algorithm yields a solution of cost 0.112, while the solution of $A^{*}_{200,000}$ costs 0.134. For this instance, $A^{*}_{200,000}$ used overestimation parameter $K = 7$ (marked in Table 2.2). Figure 2.21 shows some intermediate results obtained by $A^{*}_{200,000}$ and the greedy algorithm. Interestingly, the two methods produced the same sequence until there were 8 patches left. Then due to the overestimation, $A^{*}_{200,000}$ did some bad moves because the bad aggregation sequence still seemed better than other sequences. In contrast, the greedy algorithm was looking for locally good aggregations. Among the 32 regions that $A^{*}_{200,000}$ failed to solve optimally, solutions of the greedy algorithm cost at most 17.4% more than solutions of $A^{*}_{200,000}$; for region 155, the greedy algorithm yields a solution of cost 0.372, while the solution of $A^{*}_{200,000}$ costs 0.317 (marked in Table 2.2).

Finally, an optimal aggregation sequence of region 53 (third-last row in Table 2.2) obtained by $A^{*}_{200,000}$ is shown in Figure 2.22.

Table 2.2: The costs in detail of some regions, where $W = 200{,}000$. Parameters n and m are the numbers of patches and adjacencies on the start map, respectively. Parameter K is the overestimation factor, defined in Section 2.1. We evaluate the quality of our estimations for type change and compactness by listing the numbers $R_{\text{type}} = g_{\text{type}}(P_{\text{goal}})/h_{\text{type}}(P_{\text{start}})$ and $R_{\text{comp}} = g_{\text{comp}}(P_{\text{goal}})/h_{\text{comp}}(P_{\text{start}})$. Note that if $h_{\text{type}}(P_{\text{start}}) = 0$, then we have $g_{\text{type}}(P_{\text{goal}}) = 0$; in this case, we define $R_{\text{type}} = 1$. The marked entries are discussed in the text.

ID	n	m	K	g_{type}	g_{comp}	R_{type}	R_{comp}	Time (s)
94	32	74	15	0.029	0.266	0.135	0.531	177.9
590	30	64	15	0.216	0.273	0.164	0.510	153.0
436	27	56	15	0.273	0.330	0.439	0.550	123.3
386	26	61	15	0.280	0.296	0.279	0.474	152.6
112	26	60	15	0.216	0.306	0.173	0.490	126.3
$\vdots$	$\vdots$	$\vdots$	$\vdots$	$\vdots$	$\vdots$	$\vdots$	$\vdots$	$\vdots$
424	20	42	7	0.339	0.292	0.623	0.746	63.9
543	20	40	7	0.000	0.267	1.000	0.681	72.7
165	20	38	7	0.102	0.355	0.347	0.903	66.2
537	19	45	7	0.525	0.328	0.702	0.791	77.4
503	19	36	7	0.199	0.246	0.525	0.595	59.9
343	19	33	7	0.164	0.355	0.586	0.857	73.1
179	22	44	3	0.355	0.308	0.967	1.716	50.8
298	22	43	3	0.176	0.268	0.948	1.471	41.1
177	22	40	3	0.046	0.276	0.853	1.578	51.8
462	18	40	3	0.130	0.239	0.682	1.155	57.3
463	17	35	3	0.234	0.238	0.799	1.087	42.0
155	15	32	3	0.324	0.310	0.878	1.243	34.5
53	21	38	0	0.047	0.315	1.000	5.160	16.8
358	21	32	0	0.044	0.337	1.000	6.264	0.6
410	20	36	0	0.135	0.334	1.000	5.553	17.3
$\vdots$	$\vdots$	$\vdots$	$\vdots$	$\vdots$	$\vdots$	$\vdots$	$\vdots$	$\vdots$

2.7.2 Using Costs of Type Change and Length

We compare the greedy algorithm, A*, and ILP using $g_2(P_{t,i})$, a combination of the costs of type change and length (see Equation 2.10). For A*, we overestimated whenever we could not find a solution after having visited $W = 200{,}000$ nodes (see Section 2.5). The most time-consuming instance for A* was region 94, for which A* took 104.1 s (including repetitions) to find a feasible solution with overestimation factor $K = 31$. To avoid waiting too long, we set the time limit to 100 s for our ILP to run on one region. Note that the time limit included the time that our ILP used to set up the variables and constraints (see Sections 2.6.1 and 2.6.3). If no optimal solution was found in this time limit, a feasible solution (if found) would be returned. For some large instances, the ILP could not find any solution.

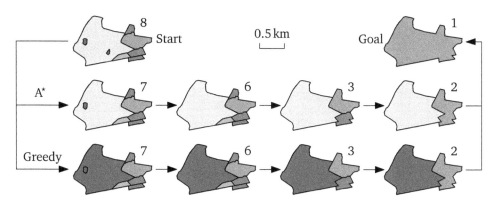

Figure 2.20: Aggregation sequences of region 85 obtained by A* and the greedy algorithm. In order to save space, we did not show the results when there are 4 or 5 patches. The numbers indicate the numbers of patches. In the sequence obtained by A*, the type of the largest polygon on the start map changed only once, which is good; while by the greedy algorithm, the type of the largest polygon changed twice.

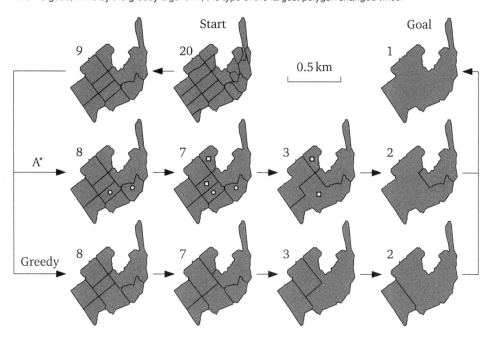

Figure 2.21: Some intermediate subdivisions of region 543 obtained by A* and the greedy algorithm. In the sequence obtained by A*, a pair of circles or a pair of squares indicates that the two parts are actually in the same patch. The numbers indicate the numbers of patches.

Using a similar format as in Table 2.1, we present the statistics in Table 2.3. A* found optimal solutions for 695 of the 734 regions (94.7%). Again, it spent most of the running time on the few regions that needed overestimation: 5.3% of the regions caused 92.3% of the total running time. The solutions by A* cost 438.2 in total, which is 3.9% less than 455.8, the total cost of the greedy algorithm.

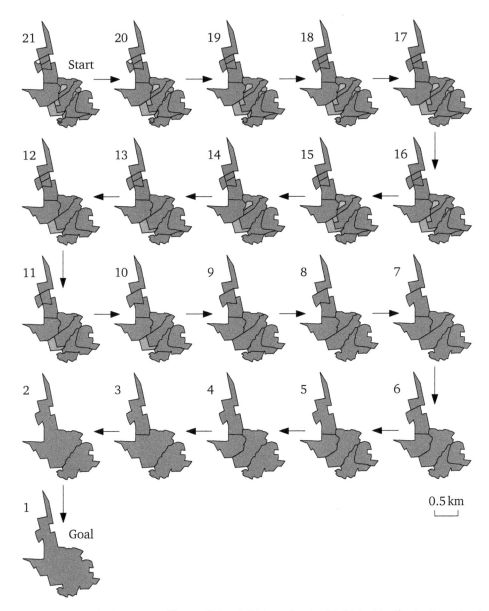

Figure 2.22: An optimal sequence of intermediate subdivisions of region 53 obtained by A* using the costs of type change and compactness. The numbers indicate the numbers of patches.

A* managed to find optimal solutions for all the regions with fewer than 15 polygons, and found only feasible solutions for the regions with more than 21 polygons. In the 39 (out of 734) regions that A* failed to solve optimally, the greedy algorithm outperformed A* for 8 regions (20.5%), which is 26.4% less comparing to the first

Table 2.3: A comparison of the greedy algorithm, the A^* algorithm, and the ILP-based algorithm when using cost function g_2 (see Equation 2.10). The notations are the same as in Table 2.1. Columns $\sum g_{\text{type}}$, $\sum g_{\text{lgth}}$, and $\sum g_2$ respectively represent the sums of $g_{\text{type}}(P_{\text{goal}})$, $g_{\text{lgth}}(P_{\text{goal}})$, and $g_2(P_{\text{goal}})$ over all the 734 instances (see Equations 2.2, 2.8, and 2.10).

Methods	#OS	#FS	k_{sum}	#nodes	#arcs	$\sum g_{\text{type}}$	$\sum g_{\text{lgth}}$	$\sum g_2$	Time (min)
Greedy	430	304 (41.4%)		$5.5 \cdot 10^3$	$4.8 \cdot 10^3$	53.0	858.5	455.8	0.1 (70.7%)
$A^*_{200,000}$	695	39 (5.3%)	150	$3.7 \cdot 10^6$	$7.3 \cdot 10^6$	52.0	824.5	438.2	44.8 (92.3%)
$\text{ILP}_{100\,s}$	449	69 (9.4%)							421.5 (27.3%)
$\text{ILP}_{200\,s}$	475	57 (7.8%)							719.2 (26.4%)

experiment (46.9%). $\text{ILP}_{100\,s}$ managed to find optimal solutions for all the regions with fewer than 8 polygons, and failed to find optimal solutions for any region with more than 8 polygons. In none of the 39 regions that A^* failed to solve optimally did $\text{ILP}_{100\,s}$ find a feasible solution. Overall, $\text{ILP}_{100\,s}$ found optimal solutions for 449 regions and found feasible solutions for 69 regions. The distributions of these regions are shown in Figures 2.23 and Figure 2.24 There are 216 regions for which our $\text{ILP}_{100\,s}$ failed to find any solution. For 22 of those regions, we did not have enough main memory to set up the variables and constraints; each of these regions has 21 polygons at least. For 67 of those regions, our $\text{ILP}_{100\,s}$ ran out of the main memory before finding any feasible solution; these regions have 14 to 20 polygons. Note that we allowed our program to use 3 GB of the main memory at most. For 123 of the 216 regions, $\text{ILP}_{100\,s}$ failed to find any solution during the time limit; these regions have 9 to 13 polygons. For the remaining 4 regions, the reason of our ILP's fail is unclear due to the fact that the solver CPLEX is like a black box for us. After we increased the time limit to 200 s for each region, $\text{ILP}_{200\,s}$ solved 475 regions to optimality, which is 26 regions more than using $\text{ILP}_{100\,s}$. Every of the 26 regions has 6 to 10 polygons. Figure 2.23 shows the percentages of the regions that are solved optimally by the three algorithms. Figure 2.24 shows the percentages of the regions that the three algorithms found feasible solutions. Figure 2.25 shows the number of regions for which the ILP found optimal, feasible, or no solutions when using the two time limits, i.e., 100 s and 200 s.

Among all the instances that were solved to optimality by A^* in both experiments (i.e., Sections 2.7.1 and 2.7.2), region 358 (marked in Table 2.2) is the largest one. In both experiments, the cost of type change is 0.044. The optimal aggregation sequences for this region obtained by using costs g_1 and g_2 are shown in Figure 2.26. We, however, noticed some unpleasant aggregates. The step from 8 patches to 7 patches when using cost function g_1 is a bad move (see Figure 2.26b). Instead we expect the result of Figure 2.26a. Using cost function g_2, we had a similar problem. The subdivision with 7 patches is such an example, where we expect the result of Figure 2.26c. In an earlier version of this chapter [see PWH17], we tried a combination of minimizing type changes and maximizing the sum of the smallest compactness values, over the whole sequence. For that objective, we had a similar problem as in

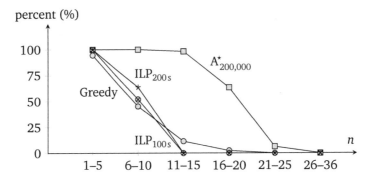

Figure 2.23: The percentage of regions that were solved optimally by the greedy algorithm, A*, and our ILP. Note that the numbers of regions according to n are shown in Figure 2.17.

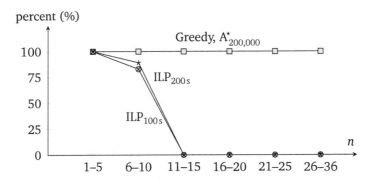

Figure 2.24: The percentage of regions for which we found at least feasible solutions by the three algorithms. Note that the numbers of regions according to n are shown in Figure 2.17.

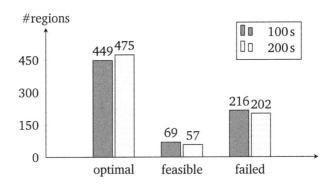

Figure 2.25: The number of regions for which our ILP found optimal, feasible, or no solutions when using time limits 100 s and 200 s. Using more time, our ILP was able to solve more instances to optimality.

Figure 2.26b. This problem, however, can be fixed easily by forbidding two patches to aggregate if their common boundary is too short. Moreover, there are two more possible solutions. First, we could integrate the shared length into our cost function, as did by van Oosterom [Oos05]. Second, we could weight the cost of shape more heavily (i.e., increasing weight factor λ of Equations 2.9 and 2.10). According to our experiences, the weight factor that we applied defines a reasonable trade-off between the different conflicting objectives, when considering a solution as a whole. However, we are far from claiming that the applied weight factor has been optimally chosen. This would probably require a user study.

2.8 Concluding Remarks

In this chapter, we investigated the problem of finding optimal sequences for area aggregation. We compared three methods to solve this problem, namely, a greedy algorithm, A*, and an ILP-based algorithm. The greedy algorithm is used as a benchmark. Unsurprisingly, it ran faster than the other two methods by far. According to our experiments, A* found area aggregation sequences with the least total cost over all regions. For some instances, however, A* had to overestimate in order to find feasible solutions. Compared to the greedy algorithm, A* reduced the total costs by 2.8% and 3.9% in the two experiments. Although the amount is small, it is worth to use A* because optimization methods can help us to evaluate the quality of a model [HW17; HS08; HW16]. For example, Figure 2.26b shows that even an *optimal* sequence can be bad. If it were not for A*, we could not tell if the bad result was caused by the greedy algorithm or the model. Because of A*, we are sure that the bad result is from our model of minimizing the type change and the compactness. The ILP-based algorithm finds optimal solutions for some regions, but for some of the other regions it cannot even find a feasible solution. Compared to the ILP-based algorithm, A* used less memory yet found optimal solutions for more regions.

Our A* has a good estimation for the cost of type change, which helps a lot to reduce the search space. Our estimation for the cost of shape (compactness or length) is poor. There are two ways to improve A* in terms of solving more instances to optimality while using the same limit of main memory. First, during the searching we can forget a node of the graph (see Figure 2.3) if all the neighbors of this node have been visited. By testing a case, we learned that half of the nodes can be forgotten during the pathfinding process. In this way, we can release some main memory and visit more nodes. Once we arrive at the goal, we know the cost for an optimal solution (the least cost). As many visited nodes have been forgotten, we do not have the shortest path so far. We need to run A* again. This time we know for sure that a path is not optimal if its cost, the sum of the exact cost and the estimated cost, is more than the least cost (of the optimal solution found previously). Consequently, we are able to prune some branches earlier than the first time we run A*. In this way, we manage to save some main memory. As a result, we are more likely to find

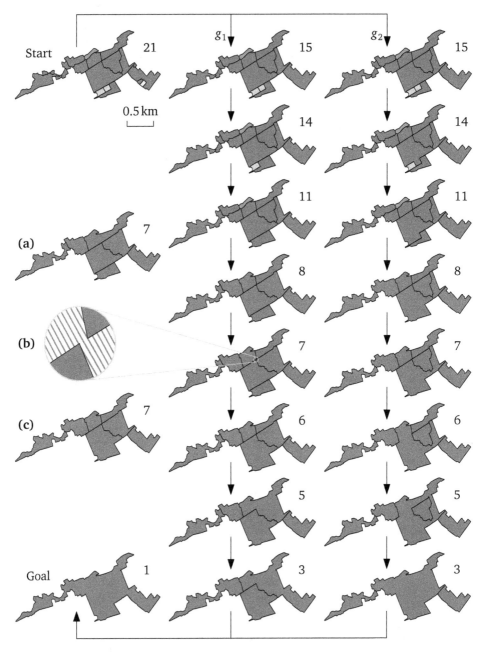

Figure 2.26: Some intermediate subdivisions of region 358 obtained by A* with different cost functions. The numbers indicate the numbers of patches. The step from 8 patches to 7 patches when using cost function g_1 is a bad move; see figure (b). Instead, we expect the result of figure (a). Using cost function g_2, we had a similar problem. The subdivision with 7 patches is such an example, where we expect the result of figure (c).

optimal solutions when the main memory is limited. Second, if we obtain a solution based on overestimation, then we know the cost of this non-optimal solution. We may decrease the overestimation factor by pruning the branches that cost more than the non-optimal solution.

We may speed up our ILP-based algorithm using a so-called cutting-plane approach as Oehrlein and Haunert [OH17]. Also, we can add more constraints to reduce the choices of variables. For example, assignment to a given center r is symmetric, hence we have

$$z_{t,p,q,r} = z_{t,q,p,r} \qquad \forall t \in T \setminus \{1,n\}, \forall p,q,r \in P.$$

Whether adding such kinds of constraints always speeds up our ILP is not clear because the solver, CPLEX, is a black box to us. Although integer linear programming may be not good at finding optimal sequences for area aggregation, it is relatively easy to formulate problems as ILPs. As stated by Cormen et al. [Cor+09, p. 861], "an efficient algorithm designed specifically for a problem will often be more efficient than linear programming both in theory and in practice. The real power of linear programming comes from the ability to solve new problems."

We may improve both the A* algorithm and the ILP-based algorithm by integrating the greedy algorithm. The idea is that we use the greedy algorithm to find a solution. Then we can use the cost of the solution as an upper bound to prune the branches of A* and the ILP. Once we see that the cost of a branch is larger than the upper bound, we can ignore that branch because it will not yield an optimal solution.

In cartography, there are many more requirements for area aggregation. For example, one requirement is to keep important land-cover areas for a longer time (such as a settlement surrounded by farmlands). This requirement can be achieved by incorporating the idea of Dilo et al. [DOH09]. They gave each type a weight, then defined the importance of a patch by the product of the area size and the type weight. While in our method, we used only the area size as importance. Another requirement is that aggregating two areas may result in an area with a generalized type, as did by van Smaalen [Sma03]. For example, aggregating *farmland* with *hedge* yields an area with type *vegetation*. In our setting, we ignored the fact that some features may inherently take linear forms (e.g., rivers). These issues can be considered in our future work.

Chapter 3

Continuously Generalizing Administrative Boundaries Based on Compatible Triangulations

Nowadays people often browse through digital maps on computers or small displays to get geographic information. To understand maps better, users interactively zoom in and out to read maps from different levels. A typical strategy to support zooming is based on a multiple representation database (MRDB). Such a database stores a discrete set of levels of detail (LODs) from which a user can query the LOD for a particular scale [HSH04]. A small set of LODs, however, leads to complex and sudden changes during zooming. Since these changes distract users, hierarchical schemes have been proposed that generalize a more-detailed representation to obtain a less-detailed one based on small incremental changes, e.g., the binary line generalisation tree (BLG-tree) [Oos05] for line simplification or the generalized area partitioning tree (GAP-tree) [Oos95] for area aggregation. Such incremental generalization processes are represented in data structures that allow users to retrieve a map at any scale. Still, the generalization process consists of discrete steps and includes abrupt changes. Discrete steps can easily cause users to lose their "mental map" during interaction, which is annoying. To support continuous zooming, van Kreveld [Kre01] proposed five ways of gradual changes, which are *moving*, *rotating*, *morphing*, *fading*, and *appearing*. These operations can be used in *continuous generalization*, which generalizes a map to obtain a sequence of maps without abrupt changes. To achieve continuous generalization, Sester and Brenner [SB04] suggested simplifying building footprints based on small incremental steps and to animate each step smoothly; Danciger et al. [Dan+09] investigated the growing of regions, meanwhile preserving their topology, area ratios, and relative positions. The strategy of using two maps at different scales to generate intermediate-scale maps has been studied in multiple representations, e.g., with respect to the selection of roads or rivers [GT14]. Actually, this strategy is a key idea of the morphing-based methods for continuous generalization. For instances, several authors have developed morphing methods for polylines [Cec03; Nöl+08; Pen+13; SH15; PDZ12; DP15] and for raster maps [RI04; Pan+09].

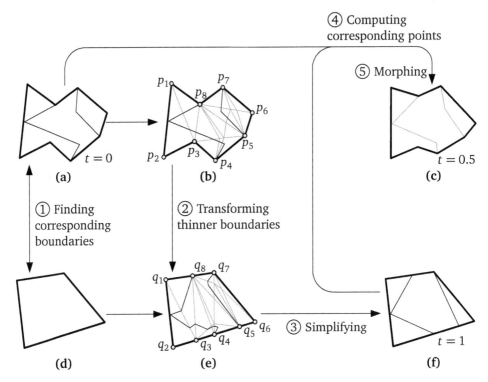

Figure 3.1: The framework of our method. The circled numbers indicate the steps. (a) The larger-scale administrative boundaries of a region. (d) The smaller-scale administrative boundaries of the same region as in (a). (b) & (e) Constructing compatible triangulations for thicker polygons in (a) and (d) in order to transform thinner boundaries in (a) to (e). (f) The thinner boundaries are simplified from the ones in (e). (c) The result of continuous generalization by morphing when $t = 0.5$. The thinner boundaries in (c) are being faded out.

Topological consistency is a property that must be attained in continuous generalization. In this chapter, we continuously generalize a two-level hierarchical subdivision—from a larger-scale map of administrative boundaries to a smaller-scale one. Our aim is to generate maps at any intermediate scales without introducing topological conflicts. For example, we try to generalize from Figure 3.1a to Figure 3.1d. Our method consists of the following five steps.

In step ①, we find corresponding boundaries between the two maps, which are the thicker polylines in Figures 3.1a and 3.1d. We call the remaining boundaries, on the larger-scale map, *unmatched* boundaries (see the thinner polylines in Figure 3.1a). In order to achieve continuous generalization, we *morph* (that is, deform continuously) between the thicker corresponding boundaries; see for example Nöllenburg et al. [Nöl+08]. The unmatched boundaries must be morphed in a way that is consistent with the thicker corresponding boundaries. As there is no correspondence for the unmatched ones, we generate the corresponding boundaries in steps ② and ③.

In step ②, we transform the thinner boundaries based on *compatible triangulations* (CTs); see Figures 3.1b and 3.1e. Two triangulations are *compatible* if they have a correspondence of their vertex sets as well as the two triangulations are topologically equivalent [SG01]. With CTs, we can transform a thinner boundary in one triangulation (see Figure 3.1b) to a boundary in the other triangulation by traversing the triangles correspondingly (see Figure 3.1e). Therefore, if there is no conflict in one triangulation, then there is no conflict in the other triangulation.

In step ③, we simplify the thinner boundaries using the Douglas–Peucker algorithm [DP73] so that the thinner boundaries have the same complexities as the thicker ones (see Figure 3.1f). We use the simplified boundaries as the correspondences for the thinner boundaries in Figure 3.1a. On this basis, we are able to morph between each pair (both thicker pairs and thinner pairs) of corresponding boundaries. Since the thinner boundaries should not stay on the smaller-scale map, we fade them out during morphing.

We compute corresponding points for each pair of corresponding boundaries in step ④, then we morph by interpolating between corresponding points in step ⑤.

In order to achieve a topologically consistent workflow, we need to make sure that any of steps ②, ③, or ⑤ must not introduce conflict. In this chapter, we concentrate on accomplishing step ②, the transformation step, without introducing topological conflicts. The topological consistency of the other two steps can be attained by employing the methods as proposed by Saalfeld [Saa99] for step ③ and Gotsman and Surazhsky [GS01] for step ⑤.

For step ②, we tested the rubber-sheeting method of Doytsher et al. [DFE01], making all vertices "influential". We soon noticed that resulting boundaries from that method often cross boundaries of the smaller-scale map. Figure 3.2 shows such an example, which corresponds to Figure 3.1e. Similar problems occurred when we applied other variants of rubber-sheeting (such as the one by Haunert [Hau05]). That is why we decided to search for a more robust method. It turned out that CTs [ASS93] can transform without introducing topological conflicts. The (quite old) idea is as follows. Suppose that point r_i is inside triangle $\triangle p_1 p_2 p_3$. Then, this point can be expressed as a *unique* convex combination of *simplicial coordinates* $\lambda_{i,1}$, $\lambda_{i,2}$, and $\lambda_{i,3}$ [Saa85]:

$$r_i = \lambda_{i,1} p_1 + \lambda_{i,2} p_2 + \lambda_{i,3} p_3,$$

where $\lambda_{i,1}$, $\lambda_{i,2}$, $\lambda_{i,3} > 0$, and $\lambda_{i,1} + \lambda_{i,2} + \lambda_{i,3} = 1$. We can *uniquely* locate r_i's corresponding point s_i in a different triangle, say, $\triangle q_1 q_2 q_3$ by using the simplicial coordinates:

$$s_i = \lambda_{i,1} q_1 + \lambda_{i,2} q_2 + \lambda_{i,3} q_3.$$

Moreover, if two distinct points r_i and r_j are in the same triangle, then we are able to locate their corresponding points s_i and s_j in another triangle such that s_i and s_j do not coincide. If points r_i and r_j are in two different triangles of a triangulation, then s_i and s_j can be located correspondingly in two triangles of the compatible triangulation. As a result, once we have CTs of two polygons, we can transform

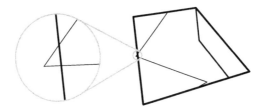

Figure 3.2: Crossings caused by the rubber-sheeting method of Doytsher et al. [DFE01].

polylines consistently (see Figures 3.1b and 3.1e). CTs have been constructed by hand in order to compare maps from different time periods Fuse and Shimizu [FS04]. By contrast, we construct CTs automatically, using the algorithm of Aronov et al. [ASS93].

Our contributions are as follows. In Section 3.1, we propose a workflow based on CTs for generalizing administrative boundaries in a continuous and topologically consistent way. We do a thorough case study for the boundaries of the counties and that of the provinces of Mainland China; we analyze the effectiveness and the efficiency of our method in Section 3.2. We conclude this chapter in Section 3.3.

3.1 Methodology

Suppose that we have two maps of administrative boundaries: M_+ and M_-. The two maps represent the same area respectively at a larger scale and a smaller scale. We use a parameter $t \in [0, 1]$ to define the process of continuous generalization. We continuously generalize from M_+ to M_- when t increases from 0 to 1.

As map M_+ is more detailed than map M_-, a region of M_- consists of several regions of M_+. Consequently, a boundary on M_- certainly has a corresponding boundary on M_+, but a boundary on M_+ may not have a correspondence on the smaller-scale map. We first find the *corresponding boundaries* on the two maps. We call the leftovers, on M_+, the *unmatched boundaries*. For a pair of corresponding boundaries, we use a dynamic programming algorithm similar to the algorithm OPT-COR [Nöl+08] to determine corresponding points. Then, we morph between corresponding boundaries by using straight-line trajectories. For an unmatched boundary, we generate its correspondence on M_-. We transform the unmatched boundary based on compatible triangulations and then simplify the new boundary using the Douglas–Peucker algorithm [DP73]. The boundary obtained from the simplification is used as the correspondence for the unmatched boundary. As a result, we are able to morph between the unmatched boundaries and the generated ones. We fade out the morphing results of the unmatched boundaries so that they will disappear when time $t = 1$.

The administrative regions are represented as polygons. An administrative region usually shares its boundary with some other administrative regions. These shared parts should be always shared even during the morphing. Furthermore, we want to avoid processing a shared boundary twice. For these reasons, we sometimes work on administrative boundaries as a set of consecutive polylines instead of polygons.

3.1.1 Finding Corresponding Polylines

We match to find corresponding polylines from map M_+ and map M_-. The basic idea of our matching is the same as the polygon-based approach of Fan et al. [Fan+16], where they matched road networks based on urban blocks. Given polygons on map M_+ and map M_-, we find corresponding polylines using three steps. Note that if the inputs are boundaries of the polygons, i.e., polylines, we can easily generate the polygons based on *doubly-connected edge list* [Ber+08, Chapter 2].

First, we copy the polygons on M_+ and merge the copied polygons according to the polygons on M_-. For each copied polygon, we try intersecting it with each polygon on M_- and record the one that has the largest intersection area. Then, we merge all the copied polygons that record the same polygon on M_-.

Second, we obtain matched polylines (i.e., corresponding polylines) respectively from the boundaries of the merged polygons and the polygons on M_-. We define that a vertex is an *intersection node* if the vertex has degree at least 3. As the merged polygons and the polygons on M_- have corresponding intersection nodes, we utilize these nodes to find corresponding polylines. We split the boundaries of the polygons at every intersection node, respectively for the merged polygons and the polygons on M_-. (Note that two polygons on the same map may share some parts of their boundaries, it is sufficient to take only one copy of the shared parts.) Then we match the split boundaries of M_+ and M_- to get corresponding polylines. We use *thicker* marks to present these corresponding polylines (see Figures 3.1a and 3.1d). Although there is a data-matching system available [see MD08], we use a simple method to attain the matching. We match the split boundaries according to their intersection areas. The buffer-based method works well in our case study as corresponding polylines have relatively close positions.

Third, we extract unmatched polylines on M_+. We split the boundaries of the polygons on M_+ at every intersection node, then we exclude all the split boundaries that overlay with the matched ones on M_+. The remained polylines are the unmatched polylines on M_+, for which we use *thinner* marks (see Figure 3.1a).

After the preprocessing, we have three types of polylines. The first one consists of the thicker (matched) polylines on M_+ (see Figure 3.1a). Each of them has a corresponding polyline on M_-. The second type consists of the thinner (unmatched) polylines on M_+ (see Figure 3.1a), each of which does not have a corresponding polyline on M_-. The third type consists of the thicker (matched) polylines on M_- (see Figure 3.1d).

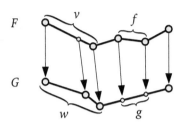

Figure 3.3: Corresponding polylines: F and G, corresponding subpolylines: v and w, and corresponding line segments: f and g.

3.1.2 Morphing a Polyline to Its Corresponding Polyline

For a pair of corresponding polylines, one being a thicker polyline on M_+ and the other being a thicker polyline on M_-, we use a variant of the dynamic programming algorithm OPTCOR of Nöllenburg et al. [Nöl+08] to compute corresponding points (possibly injecting additional vertices). The algorithm, OPTCOR, models the problem of computing corresponding points as finding an optimum correspondence, with respect to a cost function. OPTCOR considers three cases of a correspondence for an edge, namely, the edge corresponds to a vertex, to an edge, or to a merged sequence of edges. We call all the three cases corresponding subpolylines as a point or an edge can be regarded as a degenerate subpolyline.

For a pair of corresponding subpolylines, Nöllenburg et al. [Nöl+08] defined the cost as a combination of three values: (i) the average distance between the corresponding points, (ii) the length difference of the pair of subpolylines, and (iii) the changes of the vectors between corresponding points. Then, OPTCOR computes corresponding points by "looking back" to combine the last $1, 2, \ldots,$ or k edges as a subpolyline, while minimizing the cost over the whole pair of corresponding polylines. Here, parameter k gives a trade-off between quality and efficiency. It can be specified by users according to the dataset.

To make the problem simple, our variant considers only the first value in their cost, that is, the distance between corresponding points. We denote this distance by δ. In order to compute the cost function, we linearly interpolate between each pair of corresponding subpolylines so that each vertex on one subpolyline has a, possibly injected, corresponding vertex on the other one. The pairs of corresponding vertices subdivide the (sub)polylines into corresponding line segments (see Figure 3.3). A line segment is (part of) an edge of a polyline. The cost of a pair of (whole) polylines is the sum of the costs for each pair of corresponding line segments. The cost for a pair of corresponding line segments is computed as follows.

Let polyline F on M_+ and polyline G on M_- be a pair of corresponding polylines. Let $f = \overline{\alpha(0)\alpha(1)}$ be a line segment on F, and let $g = \overline{\beta(0)\beta(1)}$ be a line segment on G that corresponds to f. Let $\alpha(0) = (x_1, y_1)$, $\alpha(1) = (x_2, y_2)$, $\beta(0) = (x_3, y_3)$, and $\beta(1) = (x_4, y_4)$, which are already known. The coordinates of a pair of corresponding points $\alpha(u) \in f$ and $\beta(u) \in g$ are

$$\alpha(u) = (1-u)\alpha(0) + u\alpha(1),$$
$$\beta(u) = (1-u)\beta(0) + u\beta(1).$$

When we morph f to g, we move each point $\alpha(u)$ to its corresponding point $\beta(u)$; see Figure 3.4. We define the cost of this morphing as the integral over the distances between all the pairs of corresponding points, that is,

$$\delta(f,g) = \int_0^1 |\beta(u) - \alpha(u)| du,$$

where $|\beta(u) - \alpha(u)|$ is the Euclidean distance between $\alpha(u)$ and $\beta(u)$, which can be represented as $\sqrt{au^2 + bu + c}$. The coefficients a, b, and c are dependent on the coordinates of $\alpha(0)$, $\alpha(1)$, $\beta(0)$, and $\beta(1)$, as follows.

$$a = (x_1 - x_2 - x_3 + x_4)^2 + (y_1 - y_2 - y_3 + y_4)^2,$$
$$b = -2(x_1 - x_3)(x_1 - x_2 - x_3 + x_4)$$
$$-2(y_1 - y_3)(y_1 - y_2 - y_3 + y_4),$$
$$c = (x_1 - x_3)^2 + (y_1 - y_3)^2.$$

Let $X = au^2 + bu + c$. We have $a \geq 0$ and, since $X \geq 0$ (X is the square of a Euclidean distance), $\Delta = 4ac - b^2 \geq 0$. Note that, if $a = 0$, then $b = 0$. Let

$$\delta(f,g) = \int_0^1 |\beta(u) - \alpha(u)| du = \int_0^1 \sqrt{X} du.$$

Then $\delta(f,g)$ can be computed, according to Bronstein et al. [Bro+15, pp. 1080 and 1081, integrals 241 and 245], as follows:

$$\delta(f,g) = \begin{cases} \sqrt{c}u\big|_0^1 & \text{if } a = 0, \\ \frac{(2au+b)\sqrt{X}}{4a}\big|_0^1 & \text{if } a > 0, \Delta = 0, \\ \frac{(2au+b)\sqrt{X}}{4a}\big|_0^1 + \\ \frac{\Delta}{8a\sqrt{a}}\ln(2\sqrt{aX} + 2au + b)\big|_0^1 & \text{if } a > 0, \Delta > 0. \end{cases}$$

Cost δ can be regarded as the average distance of moving each $\alpha(u)$ to each $\beta(u)$. Figure 3.5 shows a few examples of computing δ. We obtain the optimum correspondence by minimizing the cost of moving between corresponding points, where the lengths of line segments are used as weights:

$$\delta(F,G) = \min_{\substack{\pi:\text{ correspondence} \\ \text{between } F \text{ and } G}} \sum_{\substack{f \in F \text{ and } g \in G, \\ \text{where } f \text{ corresponds to } g \text{ in } \pi}} \frac{|f| + |g|}{2} \delta(f,g).$$

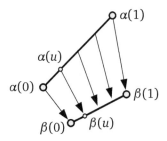

Figure 3.4: Corresponding points of a pair of corresponding line segments.

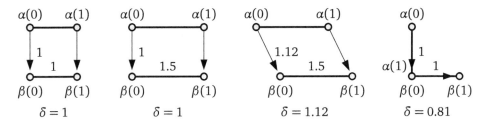

Figure 3.5: Examples of computing $\delta(f, g)$. The values in the subfigures represent the lengths of the edges.

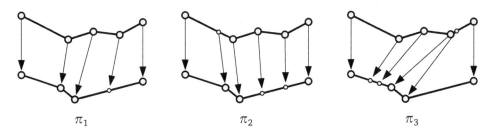

Figure 3.6: Three possible ways of defining corresponding points between the two polylines. Correspondence π_2 is the one that minimizes cost $\delta(F, G)$.

In other words, there can be many choices of defining corresponding points (see Figure 3.6), but we choose the one that minimizes cost $\delta(F, G)$.

Recall that OPTCOR considers three cases of a correspondence for an edge. We find that the first case, an edge corresponding to a vertex, may result in different numbers of vertices on the two polylines. Our major modification is removing this case from the algorithm. This change ensures that a pair of corresponding polylines will eventually have the same numbers of vertices (or line segments). This property is essential for constructing CTs, which are used later in our workflow. We name our modified version OPTCOR-S, where letter S stands for *Simplified*.

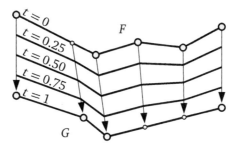

Figure 3.7: Morphing polyline F to its corresponding polyline G. The arrows show the moving trajectories of the vertices.

Suppose that there are originally n_F vertices on F and n_G vertices on G, OPTCOR-S requires that the look-back parameter k is bounded from below by n_F/n_G and n_G/n_F. Otherwise, there will be at least one segment that corresponds to a vertex. In our experiments, we always use a (large) value of k that produces results with high quality (in the sense of the dynamic-programming algorithm). We morph by interpolating between corresponding points using straight-line trajectories. Figure 3.7 shows an example with 0.25, 0.5, and 0.75 for t.

Some other algorithms for computing corresponding points can be used (e.g., linear interpolation). We observed that an algorithm which computes corresponding points more carefully can yield better results, meaning that the interpolated polylines are more similar to the two sources and crossings are less likely introduced. Some sophisticated algorithms can be considered to define the interpolation trajectories, such as geodesic shortest paths [Ber05], b-morphs [WR11], or a method based on least squares adjustment [Pen+13]. Specifically, it is possible to use CTs not only for the transformation step (as in our method) but also to ensure the topological consistency in the morphing step [see GS01; SG03; SG04].

3.1.3 Morphing a Polyline to Its Generated Corresponding Polyline During Fade-out

For the thinner polylines on M_+, morphing them must be consistent with what we do to the thicker corresponding polylines. To achieve this, we generate their corresponding polylines, that is, thinner polylines on M_-. We transform the thinner polylines on M_+ based on CTs to get a set of new polylines. Then, we simplify these new polylines to generate the thinner polylines on M_-, where we use the Douglas–Peucker algorithm [DP73].

We construct a pair of CTs for each pair of polygons correspondingly bounded by the thicker polylines on M_+ and the thicker polylines on M_- (see Figures 3.1b and 3.1e). We call them the *triangulation on M_+* and the *triangulation on M_-*. Constructing CTs requires that the two polygons have the same number of vertices, which have been attained by using OPTCOR-S (see Section 3.1.2). We use the algorithm of Aronov et al. [ASS93] to construct CTs. For the two polygons both with m vertices, we triangulate them independently (see Figures 3.8a and 3.8b). Then we create a regular m-gon and map the chords of the two triangulations into the regular m-gon (see Figures 3.8c). The mapped chords may cross with each other. We use the crossings as dummy vertices and split the mapped chords (see Figures 3.8d). As a matter of fact, these dummy vertices are called *steiner points* [ASS93]. These split chords may produce some convex faces (see Figure 3.8d). We triangulate each convex face that has more than three vertices. To triangulate, we select one vertex and add edges between this vertex to each of the other vertices, except the two immediate-neighboring ones. After triangulating, we have a *combined* triangulation (see Figure 3.8e). We map the combined triangulation (including steiner points and new edges) back to modify the two original triangulations. By the modification, we have a pair of CTs of the two original polygons (see Figures 3.8f and 3.8g).

With the CTs, we transform the thinner polylines in the triangulation on M_+ to the polylines on M_-, according to simplicial coordinates. The new polylines should traverse exactly the "same" triangles as thinner polylines on M_+. To this end, we compute the crossings between thinner polylines and the edges of the triangulation; then, we also transform these crossings into the triangulation on M_-. Because of the crossings, the new polylines have more vertices than the thicker polylines on M_+. While our aim is to generate polylines that have the same density of vertices as the thicker polylines on M_-. Hence, we simplify the new polylines (see Figure 3.1f). For a *thinner hole* (polygon) on M_-, we keep at least three vertices during simplification to avoid degenerating it to a straight line or a point. We call the simplified polylines the *thinner polylines on M_-*.

Again, we use algorithm OPTCOR-S to compute corresponding points for each pair of corresponding thinner polylines, which are respectively on M_+ and M_-. We use straight-line trajectories to interpolate between corresponding points. As the thinner polylines do not exist when $t = 1$, we fade them out during the morphing process. An example is shown in Figure 3.1c.

3.1.4 Running Time

We analyze the running time for a pair of polygons correspondingly bounded by the thicker polylines on M_+ and the thicker polylines on M_-. We use N to denote the number of vertices of the polygon on M_+, n the number of vertices of the polygon on M_-, and N' the number of vertices of all the thinner polylines inside the polygon on M_+. For simplicity, we assume that $O(N') \in O(N)$.

Constructing the CTs takes time $O(N \log N + l)$ according to Aronov et al. [ASS93], where $O(l) \in O(N^2)$ is the number of steiner points inserted during the construction. Simplifying the polylines resulted from transformation, using the Douglas–Peucker algorithm, costs time $O(N(N + l) \log N)$ [HS92]. OPTCOR-S takes time $O(k^2 N n)$ to compute corresponding points, where k is the look-back parameter. Fortunately, outputting the representation at a target scale only takes time $O(N)$. Therefore, our

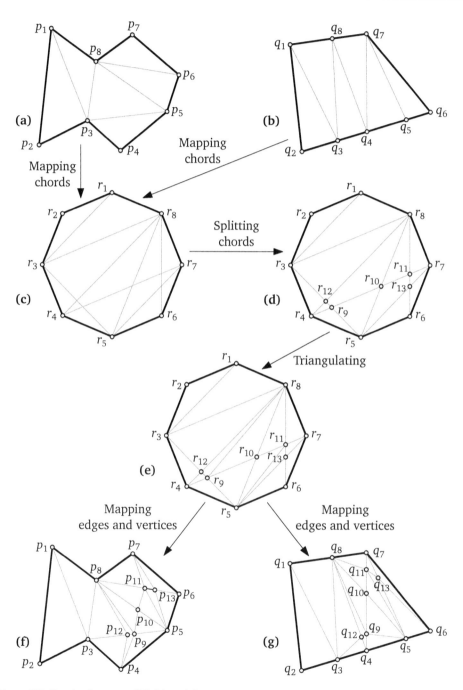

Figure 3.8: Constructing compatible triangulations.

method is feasible in real time. In fact, for each (possibly injected) vertex p on F we store a representation such as $p(t) = (1-t)p + tq$, where q is the vertex on G that corresponds to p. In our implementation, computing corresponding points is the by far most time-consuming step.

3.2 Case Study

We implemented our method based on C# (Microsoft Visual Studio 2010) and ArcGIS Engine 10.1. We ran our case study under Windows 7 on a 3.3 GHz dual core CPU with 8 GB RAM. We measured time consumption based on the built-in C# method System.Environment.TickCount.

We tested our method on the administrative boundaries of Mainland China (see Figures 3.9a and 3.9c), which are from the National Fundamental Geographic Information System and are based on the projected coordinate system *Krasovsky 1940 Lambert Conformal Conic*. We removed the enclave in Gansu province as well as all the islands. We used county boundaries (see Figure 3.9a) and provincial boundaries (see Figure 3.9c), where the polylines have been preprocessed (see Section 3.1.1). Since we can hardly see the details if we present the whole map, we focus on a small portion, say, Tianjin province[5] (also known as Tianjin municipality); see Figures 3.9b and 3.9d.

Figure 3.10 shows our results of Tianjin. Recall that our aim is to continuously generalize from counties M_+ to provinces M_-. According to the provincial boundaries in Figure 3.10c, we are able to distinguish the hierarchies of the county boundaries in Figure 3.10a Then, we find the matched polylines (the thicker ones in Figures 3.10a and 3.10c) and the unmatched polylines (the thinner ones in Figure 3.10a); see step ①.

In step ②, we transform the thinner boundaries in Figure 3.10a so that there are corresponding thinner boundaries on M_- (see Figure 3.10d). Recall that we compute corresponding points between corresponding thicker polylines using OPTCOR-S and then transform thinner polylines based on CTs. When computing corresponding points, we used the fact that the 90 thicker polylines (with 55,533 vertices) on M_+ and the 90 thicker polylines (with 7,527 vertices) on M_- shared many vertices (M_- may be generalized from M_+). We split the thicker polylines, on M_+ and M_-, into many subpolylines according to the shared vertices. We computed corresponding points for each pair of subpolylines, which was much faster than computing without the splitting. Using look-back parameter 145, the computation takes time 266 s with cost $\sum \delta(F, G) = 125{,}050 \, \text{km}^2$. Value 145 is the smallest look-back parameter that achieves the optimum result in the sense of the dynamic programming algorithm. Constructing the CTs costs 168 s. There is no conflict for the new polylines

---

[5] Please try our interactive animations of provinces Tianjin, Fujian, and Shanghai at http://www1. pub.informatik.uni-wuerzburg.de/pub/data/agile2016/. We recommend opening the website with Google Chrome.

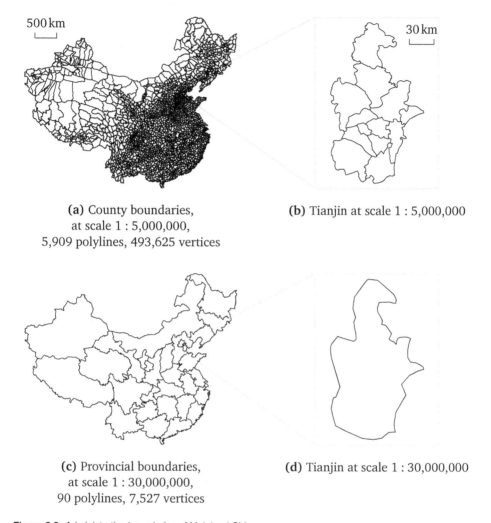

(a) County boundaries,
at scale 1 : 5,000,000,
5,909 polylines, 493,625 vertices

(b) Tianjin at scale 1 : 5,000,000

(c) Provincial boundaries,
at scale 1 : 30,000,000,
90 polylines, 7,527 vertices

(d) Tianjin at scale 1 : 30,000,000

Figure 3.9: Administrative boundaries of Mainland China.

in Figure 3.10d. However, a flaw is that there are some zigzags caused by our transformation (see for example the enlarged figure next to Figure 3.10d) We also tested transforming by the rubber-sheeting method of Doytsher et al. [DFE01], which, unfortunately, introduced 39 crossings.

In step ③, we simplified the thinner polylines in Figure 3.10d using the Douglas–Peucker algorithm. This simplification took 29 s and caused 8 crossings as well as 2 overlaps. We corrected the 10 conflicts by hand. Note that we can avoid these conflicts by using a topologically consistent line simplification method, e.g., the algorithm of Saalfeld [Saa99].

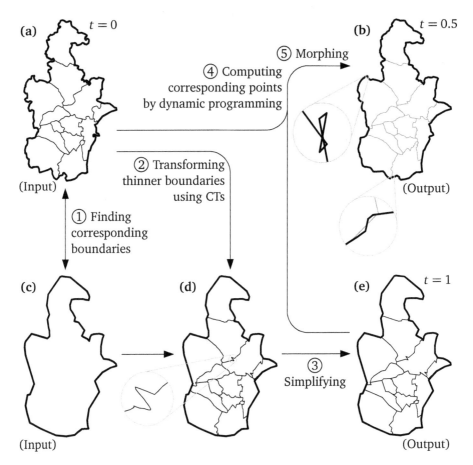

Figure 3.10: Case study on administrative boundaries of Tianjin province. The circled numbers indicate the step orders, analogous to Figure 3.1. For the sake of legibility, we did not display the CTs. Continuous generalization is achieved by morphing from (a) to (e). The thinner boundaries in (b) are being faded out during the morphing.

In step ④, we use OPTCOR-S to compute corresponding points between the 5,819 thinner polylines (with 438,092 vertices) on M_+ and the 5,819 thinner polylines (with 58,105 vertices) on M_-. This time, there are no shared vertices. The computation took about 16.5 hours with look-back parameter 203, where this value was required by a pair of corresponding polylines to guarantee $k \geq n_F/n_G$ (see Section 3.1.2). The cost for the correspondences is $\sum \delta(F,G) = 477{,}185\,\mathrm{km}^2$.

In step ⑤, we morph from counties to provinces using straight line trajectories. We show our continuous generalization of Tianjin in Figure 3.11. Generating 5,909 polylines (with 496,106 vertices) of Mainland China at any intermediate scale took about 1.5 s. Storing these polylines to shapefile format cost about 45 s, mainly due to the slow creation of polylines in ArcGIS Engine. Unfortunately, this morphing

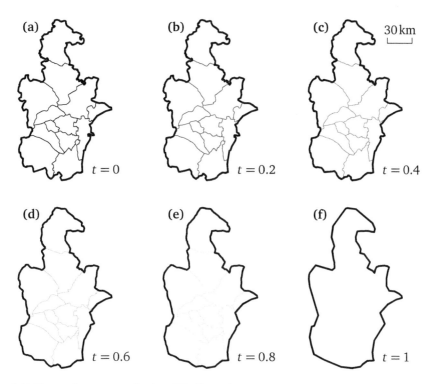

Figure 3.11: The continuous generalization of Tianjin province.

caused conflicts on the intermediate-scale maps; two examples are shown in the enlarged figures next to Figure 3.10b. For instance, there are 41 crossings on the intermediate-scale map of Mainland China when $t = 0.5$. To avoid these crossings, we can use an algorithm that guarantees topological consistency, for example, the algorithm of Gotsman and Surazhsky [GS01].

3.3 Concluding Remarks

In this chapter, we have shown that rubber-sheeting, a popular method for transforming polylines, can yield topological conflicts. Therefore, we turned to transforming based on CTs, which apparently have not been used in GIScience before, except by hand [e.g., FS04]. We have used CTs to transform unmatched polylines and managed to achieve topological consistency. Although computing corresponding points is slow, the computed results support real-time interactions, e.g., zooming. Comparing to the rubber-sheeting transformation, our method resulted in larger distortions. An extreme instance is shown in Figure 3.12. To decrease the amount of distortion, one could try constructing CTs that uses the maximum number of chords common to both independent triangulations. To that end, we could extend the dy-

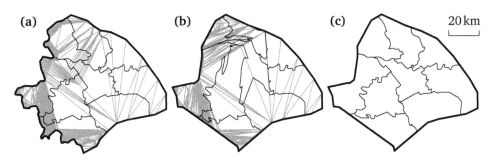

Figure 3.12: A comparison of the method based on CTs and the rubber-sheeting method for transforming the thinner polylines on M_+, using the data of Shanghai as instance. (a) M_+ and the CTs. (b) M_- and the CTs, where the thinner polylines were transformed from (a) based on CTs. (c) M_-, where the thinner were transformed from (a) by the rubber-sheeting method of Doytsher et al. [DFE01].

namic programming algorithm mentioned by Diwan et al. [Diw+11]. Whether this idea actually yields better transformation results is a question that requires further research. A similar problem is to minimize the number of steiner points when constructing CTs. This problem is NP-hard for polygons with holes and remains open for simple polygons [LM17].

Our current implementation of constructing CTs are not able to deal with holes on smaller-scale map M_-. Fortunately, Babikov et al. [BSW97] suggested a solution. We used the Douglas–Peucker algorithm to simplify the polylines resulted from transformation. As expected, this algorithm led to some topological conflicts. To solve this problem, we may use Saalfeld's variant of the Douglas–Peucker algorithm [Saa99]. In the morphing process, we have used straight-line trajectories to interpolate between corresponding points. Again, this interpolation has introduced crossings. In order to guarantee topological consistency in the morphing process, we can use an algorithm based on CTs to define the interpolation trajectories, e.g., the algorithm of Gotsman and Surazhsky [GS01]. With these two replacements, our workflow can generalize two-level hierarchical subdivisions (such as administrative boundaries) in a continuous and topologically consistent way.

Chapter 4

Continuously Generalizing Buildings to Built-up Areas by Aggregating and Growing

Digital multi-scale maps such as Google Maps and OpenStreetMap support zooming by displaying maps at different levels. This discrete strategy may result in sudden changes, which disturb user navigation. To provide better zooming experience, we try to produce a sequence of maps with small incremental changes to transit from a level to another level. This process is known as *continuous map generalization* (or continuous generalization).

A way to achieve continuous generalization is to use morphing. Often, a start map (at a larger-scale) and a goal map (at a smaller-scale) are used as input, then maps at intermediate scales are produced while the start map is morphed to the goal map. In order to morph, correspondences between two maps need to be defined. For example, corresponding points between a pair of polylines have been investigated based on dynamic programming [Nöl+08], by Delaunay triangulations and binary line generalisation tree [DP15], and by simulated annealing [Li+17]. When morphing from a point to its corresponding point, a straight-line trajectory is often used to interpolate. Peng et al. [Pen+13] defined trajectories based on least-squares adjustment in order to obtain more reasonable intermediate-scale polylines, in terms of the angles and the edge lengths. Using morphing, Peng et al. [PWH16] continuously generalized administrative boundaries based on compatible triangulations. When the numbers of line features are different on the start map and the goal map, a continuous selection is required; Chimani et al. [CDH14] proposed to generate a removing sequence applicable for road network. They removed one road at each step while keeping the remaining roads connected.

These methods are interesting but only work on lines. Our problem of building polygon interpolation cannot be achieved by similar morphings. Regarding the continuous generalization of polygon features, Danciger et al. [Dan+09] grew polygons during zooming out. Their method preserves polygons' topology, area-ratios, and relative positions. In the case where the goal map is an aggregated version of a start land-cover map, Peng et al. [PWH17] computed optimal sequences for aggregating land-cover areas.

Buildings are important elements on maps. Many methods have been proposed to generalize them but not necessarily in a continuous way. For example, Haunert and Wolff [HW10b] simplified a set of buildings based an integer program. Their simplification minimizes the number of total edges and guarantees that the errors are smaller than a user-defined tolerance. At the same time, their method does not introduce any topological conflict. Buchin et al. [BMS11] simplified buildings based on edge-move operations. Their method preserves orientations of the edges, guarantees topological correctness, and works fast.

When users zoom out on digital maps, buildings become smaller and the distances between them decrease. In addition to simplifying the buildings, we also need to aggregate them when they become too close [Wei97]. Several methods were proposed to aggregate buildings while preserving their shapes (e.g., right angles); see Regnauld [Reg01], Regnauld and Revell [RR07], and Damen et al. [DKS08]. These algorithms can be used as inspirations to define a continuous transformation of buildings.

Algorithms were also proposed to create built-up areas (that appear on our goal map) from individual buildings (that appear on our start map). For instance, Chaudhry and Mackaness [CM08] identified the boundaries of urban settlement by calculating 'citiness' based on buildings. However, it is difficult to use their method to provide a continuous transformation from buildings to built-up areas because using settlement boundaries will make the buildings lose their shapes quite fast.

Finally, some papers directly tackle the continuous transformation of buildings when scale is reduced. Li et al. [LLX17] morphed between two buildings at different scales. They managed to preserve the orthogonal characteristics of buildings, but their algorithm cannot be used in our case as our goal map does not contain buildings anymore. Touya and Dumont [TD17] transformed buildings into built-up areas, where they progressively replaced buildings by the shape of the blocks to which the buildings belong. However, this last algorithm is not continuous enough because each iteration directly transforms a set of buildings in a block to a polygon that covers the whole block. As a result, there is no existing solution for the continuous generalization of buildings into built-up areas.

Our contributions are as follows. In Section 4.1, we continuously generalize a start map of buildings (at a larger scale) to a goal map of built-up areas (at a smaller scale). The generalization consists of aggregating, growing, and simplifying. We aggregate the original buildings which will be too close at an output scale by adding bridges. We grow (bridged) original buildings by buffering, where we use so-called *miter* joins to keep the right angles of buildings. Because of using this kind of joins instead of *round* ones, we have new problems. We show how to solve these problems. We also simplify the buildings according to output scales. Finally, we analyze running time at the end of this section. We carry out a case study and discuss the performances of our method in Section 4.2. We conclude this chapter in Section 4.3.

4.1 Methodology

The input map is our start map. We denote the scale of the start map by $1 : M_s$. We generate the goal map at scale $1 : M_g$ ($M_g > M_s$) by generalizing the start map. We use time $t \in [0,1]$ to define the process of continuous generalization. We require that the generalization yields exactly the start map when $t = 0$ and the goal map when $t = 1$. The start map should be continuously changed to the goal map when t increases from 0 to 1. For the sake of convenience, we define *scale denominator* $M_t = M_s + t \cdot (M_g - M_s)$.

We carry out the continuous generalization by growing the original buildings. If some grown buildings become too close at time t, we aggregate the related original buildings by adding bridges. We grow the (bridged) original buildings by buffering with miter joins. At any time t, the grown buildings need to be simplified to look like buildings. This simplification is carried out in two steps: the first one is to use dilating and eroding to remove "dents" and "bumps"; the second step is to remove vertices using the algorithm of Imai and Iri [II88]. To make sure that buildings never shrink when t is increasing, we merge the shape of a building at time t and its shape at the preceding time (before t). We clip the buildings using the shape on the goal map to ensure that the buildings will not grow out of the intended built-up areas. Figure 4.1 shows the framework of our method; we explain the presented operators in the following subsections.

4.1.1 Growing Buildings by Buffering

We denote by d_G the *growing distance* for the goal map. At time t, the distance is

$$d_{G,t} = t \cdot d_G. \tag{4.1}$$

There are three typical joins when buffering a polygon, i.e., round, miter, and square joins (see Figure 4.2). We choose the miter joins to grow buildings in order to preserve right angles. If an angle is acute, however, an excessively long *spike* will be produced. This spike may go across other buildings (see for example Figure 4.3a). To avoid this kind of interruptions, we require that if the tip of a spike is more than $\alpha d_{G,t}$ ($\alpha \geq 1$) away from the original vertex, then we apply a *square* join (see Figure 4.3b). To keep right angles of buildings, we must have *miter limit* $\alpha \geq \sqrt{2}$. We set $\alpha = 1.5$. In this case, a square join will be applied when an angle is smaller (more acute) than 83.6°.

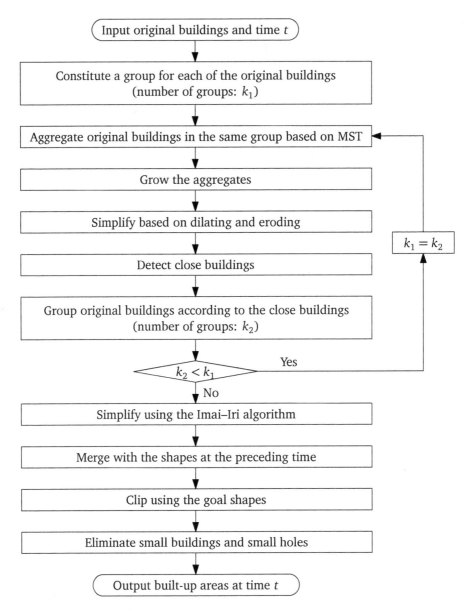

Figure 4.1: The framework of our method.

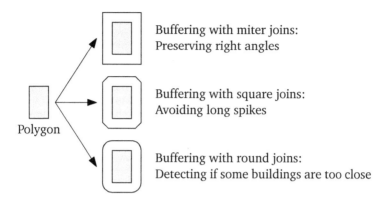

Figure 4.2: Three ways of buffering a polygon and their applications.

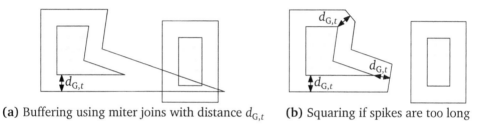

(a) Buffering using miter joins with distance $d_{G,t}$ **(b)** Squaring if spikes are too long

Figure 4.3: Using square joins instead of miter joins to avoid long spikes.

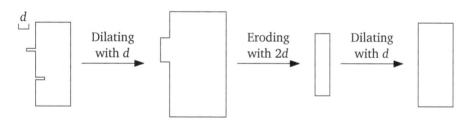

Figure 4.4: Removing dents and bumps by dilating and eroding with distance d.

4.1.2 Simplifying Grown Buildings Based on Dilating and Eroding

As mentioned earlier, methods of simplifying building have already been well studied. Damen et al. [DKS08] generalized buildings using morphological operators. A drawback of their method is that the orientation of the buildings have to be identified. Meijers [Mei16] simplified buildings using offset curves generated based on straight skeletons. Our method is similar to Meijers [Mei16]. We dilate and erode the buildings to remove dents and bumps that can occur when buildings grow (see Figure 4.4).

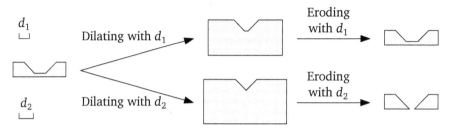

Figure 4.5: Dilating and eroding a polygon with distances d_1 and d_2, where $d_1 < d_2$. The result of using d_1 is the same as the original polygon, while the result of using d_2 become two polygons.

At time t, we should grow buildings with distance $d_{G,t}$. In order to simplify the grown buildings, we further dilate them with distance $d_{D,t}$ ($d_{D,t} > 0$), erode with $d_{D,t} + d_{E,t}$ ($d_{E,t} > 0$), and dilate back with $d_{E,t}$. A problem of this process is that a building may be split into several parts by eroding (see Figure 4.5 for example). The reason is that some parts of a building may be increased (by growing and dilating) with distance $d_{G,t} + d_{D,t}$, but can be decreased (by eroding) as much as $\alpha(d_{D,t} + d_{E,t})$. If $d_{G,t} + d_{D,t} < \alpha(d_{D,t} + d_{E,t})$ and the building is not thick enough, a thin part may disappear (see Figure 4.5 when using distance d_2). In order to avoid this problem, we require that

$$d_{G,t} + d_{D,t} \geq \alpha(d_{D,t} + d_{E,t}),$$

which means

$$d_{D,t} \leq \frac{d_{G,t} - d_{E,t}}{\alpha - 1}. \tag{4.2}$$

We would like to use $d_{E,t} = \frac{1}{2} \cdot M_t$ so that any dents and bumps narrower than l will be removed. We set $l = 0.3\,\text{mm}$ on map, which was used as a length threshold by, for example, Regnauld [Reg01]. Unfortunately, distance $d_{G,t}$ can be arbitrarily small according to Equation 4.1, but $d_{E,t}$ is at least $\frac{1}{2} M_s$. When time t is small, $d_{G,t} - d_{E,t} \leq 0$, which violates Equation 4.2, where $d_{D,t} > 0$. To mediate this violation, we set eroding distance

$$d_{E,t} = t \cdot \frac{l}{2} M_g. \tag{4.3}$$

Still, we have to make sure that $d_{G,t} - d_{E,t} > 0$, which means $t \cdot d_G - t \cdot \frac{l}{2} M_g > 0$. As a result, we need to make sure that

$$M_g < \frac{2d_G}{l}. \tag{4.4}$$

When we grow a bridged building, a "bay" may appear (see Figure 4.6b). We remove such a bay by dilating (see Figure 4.6c) and then eroding (see Figure 4.6d) with distance $d_{D,t}$. We define the width of a bay as the diameter of the largest circle that can be placed in the bay. If the width of a bay is smaller than $2d_{D,t}$, then the bay can be removed by dilating with distance $d_{D,t}$. We wish to remove bays which have

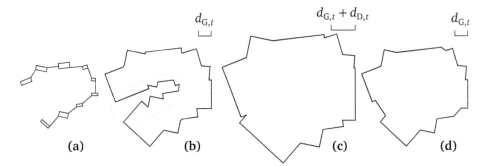

$d_{G,t}$ $d_{G,t} + d_{D,t}$ $d_{G,t}$

(a)   (b)   (c)   (d)

Figure 4.6: Removing a bay by dilating and eroding. (a) An aggregate from adding bridges (see Section 4.1.3). (b) Growing the aggregate with distance $d_{G,t}$, where the region marked by the dashed circle is a bay. (c) Dilating the grown building with $d_{D,t}$. (d) Eroding the dilated building with $d_{D,t}$.

widths less than $2r_h$. Variable $r_h = 2\sqrt{a_h/\pi}$ is the radius of a hole which is just large enough to be presented on map. Following Chaudhry and Mackaness [CM08], we set area $a_h = 8\,\text{mm}^2$ on map. Sometimes, our $d_{D,t}$ is not large enough to remove a bay with width r_h because of the limitation from Equation 4.2. Therefore, we define

$$d_{D,t} = \min(\frac{d_{G,t} - d_{E,t}}{\alpha - 1}, r_h M_t). \tag{4.5}$$

4.1.3 Iteratively Aggregating Close Buildings by Adding Bridges

We grow all the original buildings (on the start map) and, as illustrated in Section 4.1.2, simplify the grown buildings. If some buildings become too close to each other after these operations, we aggregate them by adding bridges (see for example Figure 4.7). Following Stoter et al. [Sto+09b], we define that two buildings are too close if the distance between them is less than $\varepsilon = 0.2\,\text{mm}$ on map. The real separation threshold at time t is

$$d_{\varepsilon,t} = \varepsilon \cdot M_t.$$

Our way of detecting close buildings is simple. We buffer buildings with distance $d_{\varepsilon,t}/2$ using round joins (see Figure 4.2); then, we merge the buffers that intersect with each other. On this basis, the original buildings intersecting with the same merged buffer are identified as a group of close buildings. For each pair of the original buildings in the same group, we connect them by adding a line segment to link the pair of nearest points. There can be many such line segments, and they may cross each other or may even intersect with buildings. To make the topology simple, we select only some of the line segments as *bridges*. If we consider each building as a node and each line segment as an edge, then we have a graph. By the algorithm

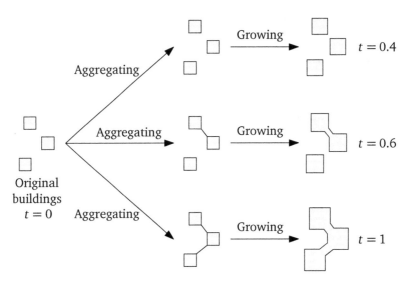

Figure 4.7: Aggregating original buildings that will become too close at a certain time by adding bridges; then, growing the bridged buildings.

of Prim [Pri57], we find a minimum spanning tree (MST) in the graph, where we use the lengths of the line segments as the weights. As a result, we use the line segments that corresponds to the edges in the MST as bridges. We aggregate the group of original buildings by adding these bridges.

Aggregated and grown buildings may become too close because of the additional bridges, so we have to iterate the aggregation process. Figure 4.8 shows such an example. We grow and buffer buildings p, q, and r. As the buffers of q and r intersect (see Figure 4.8c), we aggregate buildings q and r by adding a bridge (see Figure 4.8d). There are two buildings left in Figure 4.8d: an original one and an aggregate. We then grow and buffer the two buildings in Figure 4.8d, the buffer of building p intersects with the buffer of the bridge of buildings q and r (see Figure 4.8f). Finally, we aggregate building p with bridged q and r (see Figure 4.8g), and there is only one building left in Figure 4.8g. Then, we grow and buffer again to get the final shape of the group. As the number of buildings does not decrease from Figure 4.8g to Figure 4.8i, we stop the iteration.

When buildings have been grown and aggregated iteratively, bridges have been added. These bridges have a width of $2d_{G,t}$ (see Equation 4.1) at time t. This setting guarantees that no bridge will be thin when time $t = 1$. As we aggregated all the buildings that will become too close, all the separation distances between each pair of buildings (or aggregates) are larger than distance $d_{\varepsilon,t}$. Specifically, if a group of buildings will be aggregated at time $t = 1$, we say that these buildings are in the same *goal group*.

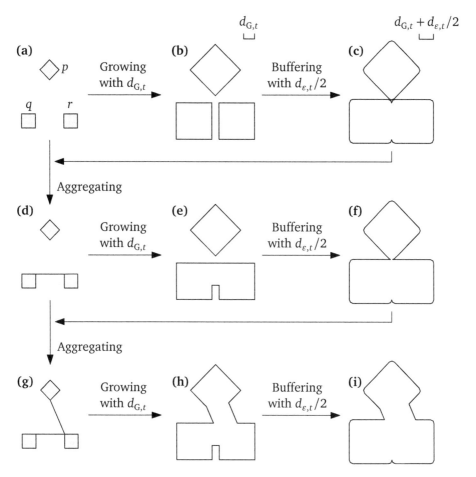

Figure 4.8: Iteratively aggregating close buildings by adding bridges.

4.1.4 Simplifying Buildings Using the Imai–Iri Algorithm

When the scale is decreasing (M_t increasing), we should remove more and more details. So, we simplify the (aggregated) grown buildings using the Imai–Iri algorithm [II88]. First, this algorithm finds all the valid shortcuts of a polyline. A shortcut is valid for a segment if the distance between the segment and the shortcut is at most a specified value (see Figure 4.9). We set the value also as $l = 0.3\,\text{mm}$ on map (see Section 4.1.2). That is, at time t, the distance threshold is

$$d_{l,t} = l \cdot M_t. \tag{4.6}$$

Second, the algorithm finds a sequence of valid shortcuts using breadth-first search. The sequence of valid shortcuts is an approximation of the polyline and has the least number of line segments, with error smaller than $d_{l,t}$.

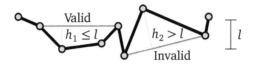

Figure 4.9: Valid and invalid shortcuts for the Imai–Iri algorithm. Parameter l is the tolerance for errors.

In order to adapt the Imai–Iri algorithm to our problem, we add two more constraints for a shortcut to be valid. One is that a shortcut must be completely inside the grown building. If a shortcut is outside, we may not be able to arrive at the shortcut by growing. The other constraint is that a shortcut is not allowed to intersect with the resulting building at the preceding time frame. We add this constraint to avoid the building to shrink.

The classical way of simplifying a polyline or a polygon is using the Douglas–Peucker algorithm [DP73]. However, it cannot simplify the shapes enough in our case. This is why we choose the Imai–Iri algorithm.

4.1.5 Generating Buildings on Intermediate-Scale Maps

Both the eroding and the line simplification may result in a building to be shrunk. Figure 4.10 and Figure 4.11 show such examples, respectively. To avoid these kinds of shrinking, for a building, we merge its shape at time t and its shape at the preceding time (before t). For example, we generate a sequence of 10 maps, which means $t \in \{0.1, 0.2, \ldots, 1\}$. Figure 4.10c shows the result at $t = 0.6$. In Figure 4.10f, the darker gray piece is included in the result at $t = 0.6$ but not in the result at $t = 0.7$. In other words, the result at $t = 0.7$ shrinks at the darker gray part. To prevent this shrinking, we merge the result at $t = 0.7$ with the result at the preceding time, i.e., $t = 0.6$. The merged result is shown in Figure 4.12a. Similarly, Figure 4.12b shows the merged result of buildings in Figure 4.11c and Figure 4.11h. This merge also avoids bridges' shrinking; Figure 4.13 shows such an example.

Added to this shrinking problem, a building aggregate on an intermediate map should never leave the goal shape of the aggregated building. Otherwise, the building will need to shrink to achieve the goal shape. To avoid shrinking, we clip the building using the goal shape and remove the parts outside.

4.1.6 Eliminating Small Buildings and Small Holes

Following the previous steps may result in some small isolated building aggregates. We should remove these small aggregates during the continuous generalization because they become too small to be visible at some point. Therefore, we eliminate a building aggregate if its area is smaller than a threshold. Following Stoter et

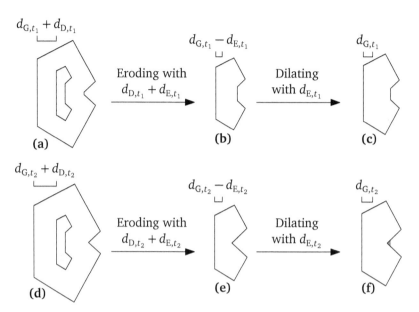

Figure 4.10: A building shrinks because of dilating and eroding, where $t_1 = 0.6$ and $t_2 = 0.7$. The gray polygons in (a) and (d) represent the original building. The transparent polygon in (a) is from growing and dilating the original building with distances d_{G,t_1} and d_{D,t_1}. The transparent polygon in (d) is obtained analogously as in (a). The darker gray piece in (f) shows the part which is included in the polygon of (c) but not in the polygon of (f).

al. [Sto+09b] and Chaudhry and Mackaness [CM08], we set this threshold to $a = 0.16\,\mathrm{mm}^2$ on map. The real threshold at time t is

$$a_t = a \cdot M_t^2.$$

For the buildings in the same goal group (see the definition in Section 4.1.3), we consider the total area of all the buildings at time t, instead of considering each building individually.

As mentioned in Section 4.1.2, we remove holes that have area less than $a_h = 8\,\mathrm{mm}^2$ on map. The real area threshold for a hole at time t is

$$a_{h,t} = a_h \cdot M_t^2.$$

4.1.7 Running Time

Suppose that our input has n edges in total. Operations like growing, dilating, eroding, merging, and clipping cost time $O(n^2)$; see Greiner and Hormann [GH98] and Palfrader and Held [PH15]. We iteratively aggregate in Section 4.1.3. In the worst case, we need to repeat $O(n)$ times, which increases our running time to $O(n^3)$. It is unlikely that we need to repeat the aggregation more than twice, though. Simplify-

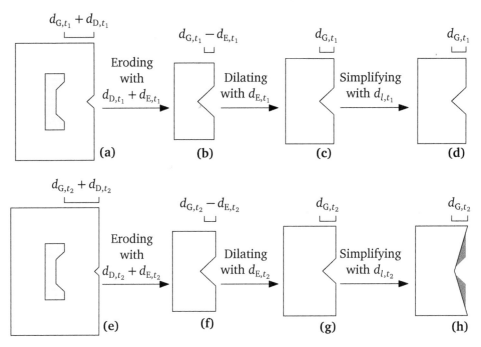

Figure 4.11: A building shrinks because of line simplification, where $t_1 = 0.7$ and $t_2 = 0.8$. The gray polygons in (a) and (e) represent the original building. The transparent polygon in (a) is from growing and dilating the original building with distances d_{G,t_1} and d_{D,t_1}. The transparent polygon in (e) is obtained analogously as in (a). Note that distances $d_{l,t_1} < d_{l,t_2}$ (see Equation 4.6); this is why the Imai–Iri algorithm does not remove any vertex of the polygon in (c) but removes two vertices of the polygon in (g). The darker gray pieces in (h) are the parts which are included in the polygon of (d) but not in the polygon of (h).

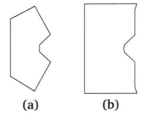

Figure 4.12: Merging a polygon with the polygon at the preceding time. (a) Merging the transparent polygons in Figures 4.10c and 4.10f. (b) Merging the transparent polygons in Figures 4.11d and 4.11h.

ing polygons using the Imai–Iri algorithm takes time $O(n^3)$. The improved version of the Imai–Iri algorithm by Chan and Chin [CC96] does not help in our case because we have more constraints when simplifying (see Section 4.1.4). As a result, the running time of our method is in $O(n^3)$.

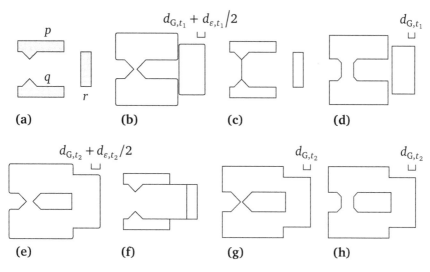

Figure 4.13: Avoiding shrinking resulted by moved bridges, where $t_1 = 0.5$ and $t_2 = 0.6$. (a) Original buildings. (b) Growing buildings with distance d_{G,t_1} and dilating with $d_{\varepsilon,t_1}/2$; buildings p and q are identified as in the same group. (c) Aggregating p and q by adding a bridge. (d) Growing the (bridged) buildings in (c) with distance d_{G,t_1}. (e) Growing original buildings with distance d_{G,t_2} and dilating with $d_{\varepsilon,t_2}/2$; all the three buildings are in the same group. (f) Aggregating by adding bridges according to the MST. (g) Growing the bridged building in (f) with distance d_{G,t_2}. The bridge in (d) shrinks comparing to (g). (h) Avoiding this shrinking at time t_2 by merging buildings in (d) and (g).

4.2   Case Study

We have implemented our method based on C# (Microsoft Visual Studio 2015) and ArcObjects SDK 10.4.1. The code is available in open source on Github[6]. The offsetting function and clipping function are available from library CLIPPER of Johnson [Joh14], which is based on the clipping algorithm of Vatti [Vat92]. The offsetting function is used for the buffering, dilating, eroding, and merging operations. We ran our case study under 64-bit Windows 7 on a 3.3 GHz dual core CPU with 8 GB RAM. We measured processing time by the built-in C# class *Stopwatch*. Our testing data is extracted from a dataset produced by the French Mapping Agency (IGN); see Figure 4.14. The data is at scale 1 : 15,000, which means $M_s = 15,000$. It represents the buildings of four towns, i.e., Aussevielle, Denguin, Poey-de-Lescar, and Siros, in the Pyrénées-Atlantiques county, south-western France. IGN also stores a dataset at scale 1 : 50,000. This dataset was obtained mostly from the data at scale 1 : 15,000 by buffering with distance 25 m, where sometimes distance 50 m was also used in order to identify towns. A restriction for the town from Boffet [Bof00] is that the longest edge in an MST of the buildings should be shorter than 100 m.

---

[6]   https://github.com/IGNF/ContinuousGeneralisation

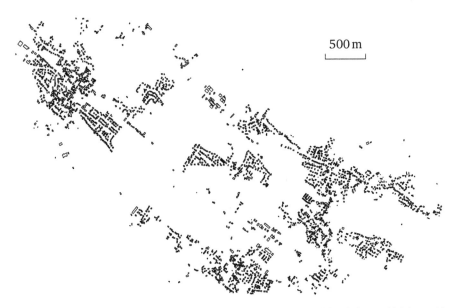

Figure 4.14: Data for our case study, at scale 1 : 15,000. There are 2,590 buildings, which in total have 19,255 edges and have area 448,802.3 m².

We set our goal scale to 1 : 50,000, which means scale denominator $M_g = 50{,}000$, and growing distance $d_G = 25$ m so that we can compare our result with the existing data. Also, this setting makes Equation 4.4 hold, where error tolerance $l = 0.3$ mm. In Equation 4.5, the first part is always smaller than the second part because of our settings. As a result, dilating distance $d_{D,t} = t \cdot 35$ m, where eroding distance $d_{E,t} = t \cdot 7.5$ m according to Equation 4.3 and miter limit $\alpha = 1.5$.

Our program took 93.6 s to compute the goal shapes of the built-up areas. The 56 built-up areas have 2,095 edges before line simplification. Using the Imai–Iri algorithm, we have 1,102 edges left. In comparison, there are 1,597 edges left when we simplified using the Douglas–Peucker algorithm.

Figure 4.15 shows the bridged original buildings as well as the goal shapes. We produced a sequence of 10 maps, i.e., $t \in \{0.1, 0.2, \ldots, 1\}$. This production cost 668.2 s in total. We show such a sequence of maps in Figure 4.16 for marked region R_1 in Figure 4.15. The sequence of maps grows continuously, and the intermediate results well reflect the pattern of the original buildings. Unfortunately, our method produced lengthy building aggregates, which may annoy users. Some examples can be found in Figure 4.17 when time $t = 0.3$. To avoid this problem, we could restrict the number of nodes when we group buildings based on an MST. Using this restriction, however, we will not be able to guarantee that the distance between any two (aggregated) buildings is larger than distance threshold $d_{l,t}$ (see Equation 4.6).

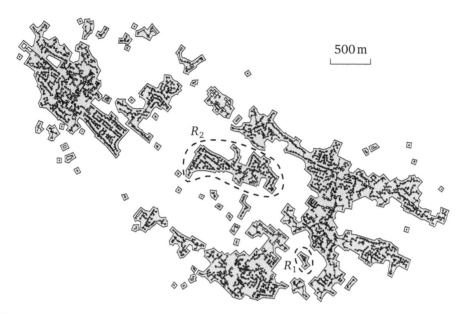

Figure 4.15: Bridged original buildings and goal shapes (darker polygons), without eliminating small buildings and holes, where the goal shapes are for scale 1 : 50,000. There are 56 goal shapes, which have 1,135 edges in total.

We counted the numbers of buildings in our results and compared them to the numbers calculated by the radical law of Töpfer and Pillewizer [TP66]; see Figure 4.18. We have exaggerated-area symbols; so we use C_{b3} and C_{z3} for Equation 2 of Töpfer and Pillewizer [TP66]. As a result, we computed the numbers according to

$$n_t = n_s \left(\frac{M_s}{M_t} \right)^2, \tag{4.7}$$

where $n_s = 2,590$ is the number of buildings on start map and n_t is the number of buildings on the map at scale 1 : M_t. Equation 4.7 is intuitive because it demonstrates that the number of buildings in a unit area on map should be fixed. According to Figure 4.18, our numbers decrease faster than the numbers computed by the radical law. Still, the radical law seems to agree with our results.

We also compared the areas on map of our results with the areas computed by the radical law of Töpfer and Pillewizer [TP66]. Our data, at scale 1 : 15,000, has area 448,802.3 m^2, which is 1,994.7 mm^2 on map. The radical law concerns about the number of objects, so we slightly abuse the law. In Equation 4.7, we replace the number with area and have

$$A_t = A_s \left(\frac{M_s}{M_t} \right)^2.$$

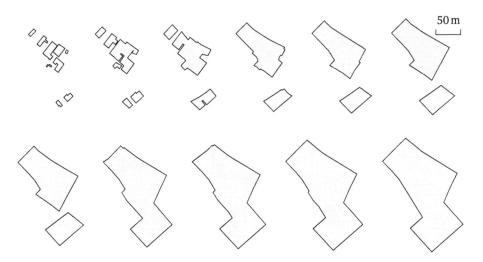

Figure 4.16: A sequence of maps at time $t \in \{0, 0.1, 0.2, \ldots, 1\}$ of marked region R_1 in Figure 4.15.

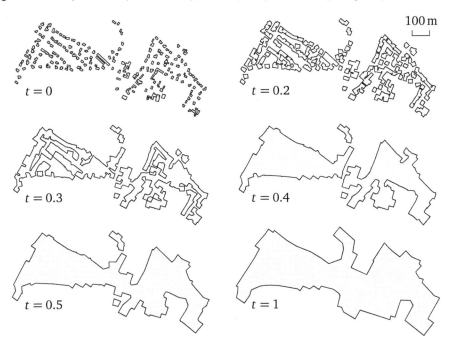

Figure 4.17: Some intermediate-scale results of marked region R_2 in Figure 4.15. When time $t = 0.3$, there are some lengthy aggregates.

The comparison is shown in Figure 4.19. The area on map of our results increases from time $t = 0$ to time $t = 0.4$. The reason is that there are many bridges appearing during this period. Comparing the two curves in Figure 4.19, we see a disagreement between the radical law and our results.

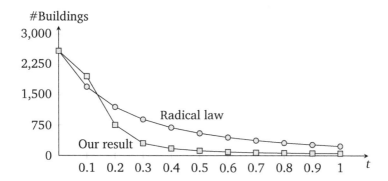

Figure 4.18: A comparison of the numbers of buildings between our result and the radical law.

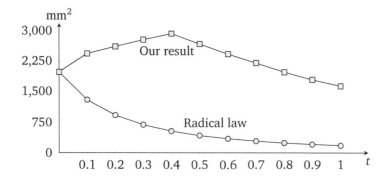

Figure 4.19: A comparison of the total area on map of buildings between our result and the radical law.

In Figure 4.20, we show our built-up areas at time $t = 1$ (dark polygons) and the data at scale 1 : 50,000 from IGN (transparent polygons). No small building was removed in our result or the IGN data. The boundaries of our built-up areas are more straight than that of the IGN data. We have 1,135 edges, while the IGN data has 4,968 edges. From this perspective, our result is more reasonable than the existing data. A questionnaire, however, is needed to make a more convincing comparison.

4.3   Concluding Remarks

We proposed a method to continuously generalize buildings to built-up areas by aggregating and growing. We managed to produce a sequence of maps in which the buildings are always growing and, at the same time, are simplified. Our method, however, may produce lengthy aggregates. For the goal map at scale 1 : 50,000, the shapes of our built-up areas are more reasonable than the data from IGN.

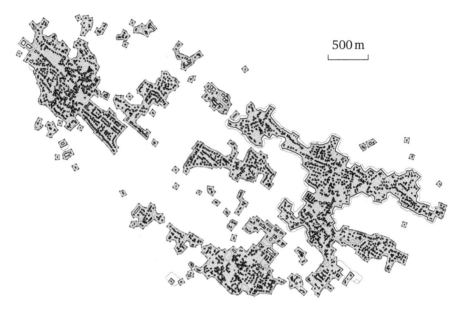

500 m

Figure 4.20: A comparison of our built-up areas at time $t = 1$ and the data from IGN at scale $1 : 50,000$ (transparent polygons). Some built-up areas from IGN are split because of streets' crossing.

It is always interesting to know the quantity that we should keep on a map. We compared the numbers of buildings, and it is quite consistent with the radical law of Töpfer and Pillewizer [TP66]. We also compared the areas of our results and the values computed by our variant of the radical law. The difference between them is large. Eventually, our result is a set of settlement boundaries. An interesting problem is to compare our method with Chaudhry and Mackaness [CM08]. Our method is supposed to provide a smooth transition between the representation of individual buildings and that of built-up areas, but the only way to verify that smoothness is to carry out a user survey. In the survey, we should compare our approach to non-continuous generalization approaches.

Chapter 5

Morphing Polylines
Based on Least-Squares Adjustment

Digital maps such as Google Maps or OpenStreetMap have become important sources of geographic information. When users interactively browse through such maps on computers or small displays, they often need to zoom in and out to get the information desired. Often, zooming is supported by a multiple representation database (MRDB). This database stores a discrete set of levels of detail (LODs), from which a user can query the LOD for a particular scale [HSH04]. A small set of LODs, however, leads to large and sudden changes during zooming, which distracts users. Therefore, hierarchical schemes have been proposed that implement the generalization process based on small incremental changes, for example, the binary line generalization tree (BLG-tree) [Oos05] for line simplification or the generalized area partitioning tree (GAP-tree) [Oos95] for area aggregation. The incremental generalization process is represented in a data structure that allows a user to retrieve a map at any desired scale. Still, the generalization process consists of discrete steps and includes abrupt changes. To achieve a continuous generalization, Sester and Brenner [SB04] simplified building footprints based on small incremental steps and smoothly animated each step. Also aiming at a continuous generalization, several authors have developed methods for morphing between two polylines [Cec03; Nöl+08]. Most of these methods consist of two steps [Cec03; Nöl+08; PDZ12]. The first step is to compute the corresponding points of the two polylines. The second step is to define a trajectory for each pair of corresponding points. Most often, straight lines are used as trajectories. Then, morphing is realized by moving points along the straight-line trajectories with constant speeds.

In this chapter, we relax the requirement of using straight-line trajectories for morphing. Our concern with straight-line trajectories is that characteristics (e.g., bends) of the polylines can change drastically during a morphing process. To better keep the characteristics, we suggest that the angles and the edge lengths of polylines should change linearly during a morphing process. As Figures 5.1a and 5.1b show, this is clearly not accomplished with straight-line trajectories. In contrast, the new method that we present in this chapter yields a close-to-linear relationship, for example, between time and edge lengths; see Figures 5.1c and 5.1d.

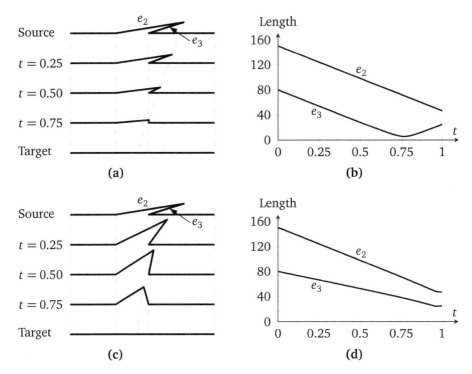

Figure 5.1: Morphing between a source polyline and a target polyline. When morphing based on straight-line trajectories (a), edge e_3 receives almost zero length at time $t = 0.75$ and then grows again (b). With our method (c), the edge lengths change almost linearly (d).

The chapter is organized as follows. We review related work in Section 5.1. The details of our method are presented in Section 5.2, which include soft constraints, hard constraints, estimates for the unknowns, and the iterative process of our method. We present a case study in Section 5.3.2, which shows that our method generally performs well but also reveals new problems. We conclude the chapter in Section 5.4.

5.1 Related Work

Different methods of morphing have been developed for map generalization. In map generalization, there are many constraints that need to be satisfied [Har99]. These constraints should also be satisfied by intermediate-scale features displayed when morphing. According to van Kreveld [Kre01], the amount of displacement between the corresponding vertices of two maps at different scales is quite small; thus, when using straight-line trajectories for morphing, hardly any features will be in conflict with the interpolated features. We, however, argue that even in simple situations, such as the one in Figures 5.1a and 5.1b, straight-line trajectories fail to generate satisfactory intermediate-scale features. In fact, there are methods that use curves rather than straight lines as vertex trajectories, for example, circular arcs or parabolas [WR09]. In contrast to these methods, our method does not require the trajectories to be of any particular curve type. Instead, we define the morphing process based on constraints that we impose on the features at intermediate scales.

Intermediate features are expected to be similar to the source feature and the target feature. We consider the angles and the edge lengths to be very important attributes of a feature, at least because similarity measures are often defined based on the angles and the edge lengths; [e.g., Ark+91; LL00; FE06]. Sederberg et al. [Sed+93] morphed two polygons by changing the angles and the edge lengths linearly over time. The authors also showed how to tweak the edge lengths and/or the angles to guarantee that the intermediate polygon is closed at any time. We use an approach similar to Sederberg et al. [Sed+93]. We also try to achieve that the angles and the edge lengths change linearly. Unlike Sederberg et al. [Sed+93], however, we simultaneously handle multiple constraints by defining (and solving) the model of a least-squares adjustment. A completely different approach was taken by Connelly et al. [CDR03]. They proved that any polyline can be straightened, that is, the vertices can be moved to a straight line such that the edge lengths never change and the edges never intersect. Streinu [Str00] showed that a quadratic number of moves suffices and presented how to compute those. However, in order to morph a polyline into another polyline (with the same edge lengths), Streinu [Str00] would morph the former into a straight line and then into the latter. Thereby, that method will significantly change the angles.

Least-squares adjustment (LSA) has been shown to be effective in handling multiple constraints in map generalization [Ses00; HS02]. Basically, it relies on function $\phi : R^u \to R^m$ that defines the relationship between vector $\hat{X}$ of u *unknowns* and vector L of m *observations*. Given function ϕ and vector L, it is reasonable to ask for vector $\hat{X}$ that strictly satisfies $L = \phi(\hat{X})$. Such a vector, however, normally does not exist since m is usually larger than u. Therefore, the *corrections for observations*, vector v, is introduced. Then, our aim is to find $\hat{X}$ and v such that

$$L + v = \phi(\hat{X}),$$

and $v^T P v$ is minimal, where P is a matrix that allows us to set weights to observations. LSA is particularly easy to solve if a linear relationship between the unknowns and the observations exists, that is,

$$\phi(\hat{X}) = A\hat{X} + d, \tag{5.1}$$

where both matrix A and vector d have constant values. An optimum solution is given with

$$\hat{X} = X_0 + (A^T P A)^{-1} A^T P l, \tag{5.2}$$

where *estimates* X_0 can be any vector of dimension u and vector $l = L - \phi(X_0)$.

If the relationship between the unknowns and the observations is not linear, then we have to compute iteratively in order to find an approximation of vector $\hat{X}$. In this case, matrix A is defined based on the partial derivatives of function ϕ at X_0. Usually, Equation 5.2 yields an approximation of the optimum unknown vector that is better than X_0. A good approximation of $\hat{X}$ can be found by iteratively solving Equation 5.2. In each iteration (except the first), we assign the newly computed vector, $\hat{X}$, to vector X_0. Before we start the iteration, we should choose a set of initial estimates that is close to $\hat{X}$. The smaller the difference between X_0 and $\hat{X}$ is, the more likely we find an approximation of $\hat{X}$.

Since eighty percent of all objects (points, lines, and areas) in a typical medium-scale topographic map consist of lines [Mul91], we focus on morphing polylines in this chapter.

5.2 Methodology

In this section, we present our LSA-based morphing method. We introduce some definitions in Section 5.2.1. Then, we model multiple requirements as constraints. The soft constraints are presented in Section 5.2.2. We set constant values to the coordinates of some vertices to implement hard constraints in Section 5.2.3. The estimates for the unknowns are given in Section 5.2.5. Finally, we sketch the stop condition of the model in Section 5.2.6.

5.2.1 Preliminaries

Suppose that we have polyline B with vertices $b_1, \ldots, b_M$ and polyline C with vertices $c_1, \ldots, c_N$, where B and C represent the same geographic feature. Vertices b_1 and c_1 as well as b_M and c_N correspond to each other (see Figure 5.2a). For every vertex of B, we find a corresponding point (not necessarily a vertex) on C, and vice versa. As a result, we have two new polylines, i.e., B' and C', which have the same number, say n, of vertices (see Figure 5.2b). How to find the corresponding pairs of vertices is not discussed in this chapter. We apply a dynamic-programming algorithm similar to Nöllenburg et al. [Nöl+08], but any other method could be used as well.

The morphing process starts at time $t = 0$, from polyline B', and ends at time $t = 1$, to polyline C'. Generally, we denote the polyline displayed at time t by $D(t)$, thus $D(0) = B'$ and $D(1) = C'$. We denote the i-th vertex of $D(t)$ by $d_i(t)$.

5.2.2 Soft Constraints

We compute polyline $D(t)$ by constraining its angles and the lengths of its edges. That is, for each angle and each edge length, we define an expected value, which is an *observation* in LSA. In most cases, these expected values cannot be achieved at the same time because they may contradict with each other. Therefore, we require

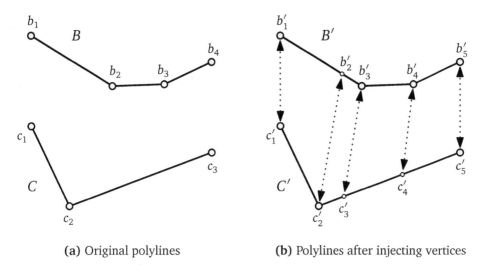

(a) Original polylines   (b) Polylines after injecting vertices

Figure 5.2: Illustration of corresponding vertices.

that the computed angles and edge lengths are close to the expected values. More precisely, we obtain the differences between the computed values and the expected values, then we square the differences and sum up the squares; we want to minimize the sum. These requirements for angles and edge lengths constitute soft constraints in our method. In order to make polylines behave as in our motivating example (see Figures 5.1c and 5.1d), we define the expected values by a linear interpolation between the values of the source polyline and the target polyline. For the angles, the expected values are

$$\beta_i(t) = (1 - t) \cdot \beta_i(0) + t \cdot \beta_i(1), \tag{5.3}$$

where $i = 2, \ldots, n - 1$. Angles $\beta_i(0)$ and $\beta_i(1)$ are respectively from polylines B' and C' (see Figure 5.3).

Similarly, for the edge lengths, we define

$$l_i(t) = (1 - t) \cdot l_i(0) + t \cdot l_i(1), \tag{5.4}$$

where $i = 1, \ldots, n - 1$. Lengths $l_i(0)$ and $l_i(1)$ are respectively from polylines B' and C' (see Figure 5.3).

By applying LSA, our aim is to compute the adjusted coordinates of the vertices for polyline $D(t)$. Therefore, we need to express the relationships between the adjusted coordinates, $\hat{x}_1(t), \hat{y}_1(t), \ldots, \hat{x}_n(t), \hat{y}_n(t)$, and the observations (i.e., the expected angles and the expected edge lengths). In other words, the adjusted coordinates are our *unknowns* for LSA. In the following, we express the relationships.

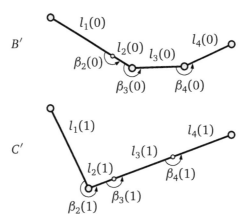

Figure 5.3: Illustration of initials and finals.

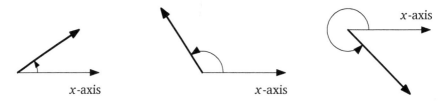

Figure 5.4: The x-axis angles of some edges. The thin line segments represent x-axes, and the thick ones represent some edges.

Angles: Angle $\beta_i(t)$ can be computed based on the difference between edge e_{i-1}'s x-axis angle and edge e_i's x-axis angle. The x-axis angle of an edge is the angle that we rotate x-axis until it is parallel to the edge (see some examples in Figure 5.4). Depending on the quadrants in which e_{i-1} and e_i lie relative to the vertex $d_i(t)$, a multiple of π has to be added. As a result, for the adjusted angle $\hat{\beta}_i(t)$ of observation $\beta_i(t)$, we require that

$$\hat{\beta}_i(t) = \arctan \frac{\hat{y}_{i+1}(t) - \hat{y}_i(t)}{\hat{x}_{i+1}(t) - \hat{x}_i(t)} - \arctan \frac{\hat{y}_i(t) - \hat{y}_{i-1}(t)}{\hat{x}_i(t) - \hat{x}_{i-1}(t)} + K_i \cdot \pi, \qquad (5.5)$$

where $K_i \in \mathbb{Z}$ is a constant that only depends on i. For the LSA, we have to compute the partial derivatives of $\hat{\beta}_i(t)$ with respect to the unknowns. These partial derivatives do not depend on the constant term $K_i \cdot \pi$. Therefore, we can neglect it.

Edge lengths: Each edge length is a Euclidean distance. Hence, for adjusted edge length $\hat{l}_i(t)$, we require that

$$\hat{l}_i(t) = \sqrt{(\hat{x}_{i+1}(t) - \hat{x}_i(t))^2 + (\hat{y}_{i+1}(t) - \hat{y}_i(t))^2}. \qquad (5.6)$$

Here, Equations 5.5 and 5.6 constitute function $\phi(\hat{X})$; see Equation 5.1. Since functions $\hat{\beta}_i$ and $\hat{l}_i$ are not linear, we have to linearize them by computing partial derivatives [Ses00; HS02].

Without adding hard constraints to our model, there is no need for an adjustment. We can perfectly satisfy every soft constraint simply by creating a new polyline with the expected angles and the expected edge lengths. However, the new polyline can be very different from our source polyline and target polyline; in order to avoid this problem, we add hard constraints of prescribing some end vertices of the new polyline.

5.2.3 Hard Constraints

There may be some common characteristic vertices on polylines B' and C'. These vertices should be kept during morphing. If we have vertices $d_i(0) = d_i(1)$ for some $i \in \{1, \ldots, n\}$, we require as hard constraints that vertices $d_i(0) = d_i(t) = d_i(1)$ for time $t \in [0,1]$. That is to say, for these characteristic vertices, we do not introduce unknowns in the LSA. Note that our method does not require the existence of such common characteristic vertices, but it can handle them.

Even if vertex $d_i(0)$, on polyline B', does not have the exact same position as its corresponding vertex $d_i(1)$, on polyline C', we may want to constrain computed vertex $d_i(t)$ to lie at a prescribed position. In particular, by prescribing the end vertices of some polylines that meet each other at these end vertices, we can guarantee that these polylines always meet each other. This is useful if we need to deal with a geometric graph that, for example, represents a road network. We suggest prescribing the vertices with degree higher than two (e.g., road junctions), which allows us to treat each path between two such vertices as an independent problem. When prescribing vertex $d_i(t)$, we apply a simple linear interpolation between vertices $d_i(0)$ and $d_i(1)$. That is, we set

$$\begin{pmatrix} x_i(t) \\ y_i(t) \end{pmatrix} = (1-t) \cdot \begin{pmatrix} x_i(0) \\ y_i(0) \end{pmatrix} + t \cdot \begin{pmatrix} x_i(1) \\ y_i(1) \end{pmatrix},$$

where $x_i(t)$ and $y_i(t)$ are the x- and y-coordinates of $d_i(t)$. However, we should not constrain too many vertices this way; otherwise, we will achieve no improvement compared to the existing method based on straight-line trajectories.

We note that some additional hard constraints may be needed. For example, we may want to remain some right angles when morphing for buildings. However, we do not handle those kinds of hard constraints in this chapter.

5.2.4 Weights

For simplicity, we set the weight for each edge length as 1. Because angles are sensitive to coordinates' changes (see Figure 5.5 for example), we give angles larger weights in order to make them stable. An angle can suddenly change as much as radian 2π. We assign weight $4\pi^2$ to angles because we are dealing with squares. Our weights for angles and edge lengths constitute a diagonal matrix, that is,

$$P = \operatorname{diag}(4\pi^2, \ldots, 4\pi^2, 1, \ldots, 1).$$

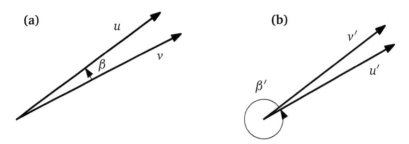

Figure 5.5: Angle is sensitive to the changes of coordinates. (a) Vector v, vector v, and the angle between them, β. (b) Because of adjustments, we have two new vectors v' and u', where the angle has been significantly changed (see β').

5.2.5 Estimates

To define the morphing process, we compute k intermediate polylines, where parameter k should be large enough to give a smooth animation. We define each step to take the same amount of time; in the i-th step, $t = \frac{i}{k+1}$. We compute polylines $D(\frac{1}{k+1}), D(\frac{2}{k+1}), \ldots, D(\frac{k}{k+1})$ in succession. Since the polyline at time $\frac{i}{k+1}$ will be similar to the polyline at time $\frac{i-1}{k+1}$, we use the vertex coordinates of the precedingly computed polyline as estimates for the unknowns in the LSA.

5.2.6 Iterative Process

Since our model contains non-linear constraints (see Equations 5.5 and 5.6), we need to solve it iteratively. We define the *corrections of the coordinates* as

$$\hat{x}(t) = (A^{\mathrm{T}}PA)^{-1}A^{\mathrm{T}}Pl. \tag{5.7}$$

We compute $\hat{X}$, which represents angles and edge lengths of a polyline, by Equation 5.2. If the norm of corrections $\hat{x}(t)$ is larger than a user-set threshold, we use the computed $\hat{X}$ as new X_0 and then compute again by Equation 5.2, also with new l. We iterate this process until the norm of vector $\hat{x}(t)$ is small enough.

5.3 Case Study

To get reasonable corresponding points between two polylines that will be morphed, we used a dynamic-programming algorithm similar to that of Nöllenburg et al. [Nöl+08]. Their algorithm uses characteristic vertices (in our experiments, all the vertices are regarded as characteristic vertices) and segments between consecutive characteristic vertices as elements to match to minimize a defined cost function. To make the soft constraints of angles meaningful, we always prescribe the first two vertices and the last two vertices of the polylines.

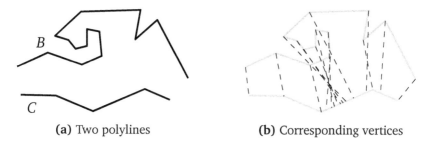

(a) Two polylines   (b) Corresponding vertices

Figure 5.6: An artificial data used in our case study.

5.3.1 Case Study on Artificial Data

We tested our method on an instance from Bereg [Ber05]; see Figure 5.6. The corresponding vertices computed by the dynamic-programming algorithm (see Section 5.2.1) are shown in Figure 5.6b. Figure 5.7 shows the results of morphing from polyline B to polyline C based on straight-line trajectories and our LSA, respectively. Based on straight-line trajectories, the left part of the "bend" shrinks, and a self-intersection occurs at time $t = 0.75$. While based on LSA, the same part of the bend moves to the right side and then moves to the target edges. Therefore, our method is more reasonable.

Unfortunately, there are still problems with our method. First, if we define the corresponding vertices between the polylines with a simple linear interpolation algorithm (as shown in Figure 5.8a), then we obtain undesirable results when morphing polyline C to polyline B based on LSA. Figure 5.8b shows that the "interpolated line" jumped below polyline C.

Second, we may have self-intersections for some instances. Figure 5.9 shows such an example, where we have several self-intersections at time $t = 0.5$. This is because that we do not have a mechanism to guarantee topological correctness of generated polylines.

Third, sometimes the iterative process (see Section 5.2.6) does not stop because the norm of corrections $\hat{x}(t)$ (see Equation 5.7) does not converge to value 0. The reason is probably that the polylines contain very short edges. Figure 5.10 shows such a strange result. For the corresponding vertices shown in Figure 5.9b, we add an extra pair of corresponding vertices presented by the black curve in Figure 5.10a. The two extra vertices are very close to one of the pairs of corresponding vertices. Now, we have a pair of very short corresponding segments. Because of that, our LSA generated a strange polyline at time $t = 0.83$. Figure 5.10b shows the result, where the circle represents the extra vertex on the strage polyline. By comparison, our LSA generated a correct polyline when we did not add the extra pair of vertices. Figure 5.10c shows the result, where the square represents the extra vertex on the correct polyline. Moreover, our LSA does not converge at time $t = 0.90$ when we have the extra vertices.

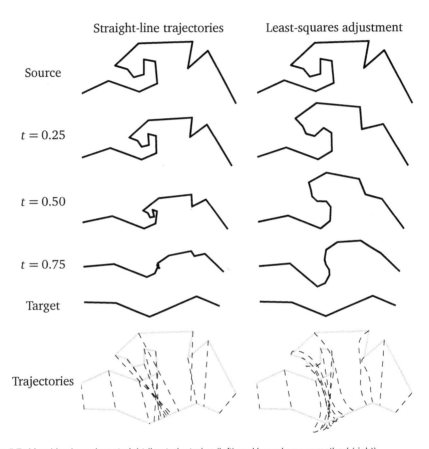

Figure 5.7: Morphing based on straight-line trajectories (left) and based on our method (right).

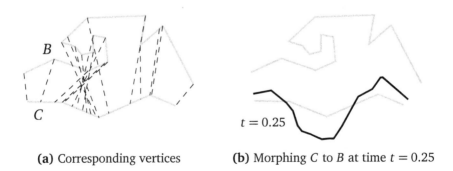

(a) Corresponding vertices   (b) Morphing C to B at time $t = 0.25$

Figure 5.8: An undesirable result based on our LSA.

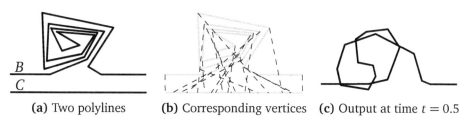

| **(a)** Two polylines | **(b)** Corresponding vertices | **(c)** Output at time $t = 0.5$ |

Figure 5.9: Some self-intersections generated by our LSA.

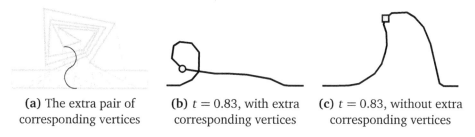

| **(a)** The extra pair of corresponding vertices | **(b)** $t = 0.83$, with extra corresponding vertices | **(c)** $t = 0.83$, without extra corresponding vertices |

Figure 5.10: A strange result by our LSA.

5.3.2 Case Study on Real-World Data

We tested our method on a part of the coastline of China (Figures 5.11a and 5.11d). The scale of the source polyline is 1 : 5,000,000, the length is 1,002 km, and the number of vertices is 233; the scale of the target polyline is 1 : 30,000,000, the length is 605 km, and the number of vertices is 66. Figures 5.11b and 5.11c show the morphing results at times $t = 0.25$ and $t = 0.75$, where the prescribed vertices are marked by dots. Overall, we got nice results, but there are still some problems. In region R_1, the two segments almost intersect at time $t = 0.25$; in region R_2, the "bend" first expands and then shrinks. The two phenomena are not appropriate. There are two reasons for both problems. First, the changes (decrease or increase) of the angles are faster than needed. Second, the decreases of the lengths are slower than needed. Both reasons tend to make a bend expand and then shrink. To solve this problem, we need a better model to simulate the changes of angles and edge lengths, rather than use Equations 5.3 and 5.4.

5.4 Concluding Remarks

We have introduced a method for morphing polylines that tries to linearly change the angles and the edge lengths over time. Our approach is based on LSA and can handle soft and hard constraints. Our first results are promising. Still, there are open problems. In particular, we have to ensure that our method always converges to a good solution. We also aim to model more constraints, for example, to avoid self-intersections. Besides, a further topic is to combine morphing and simplification.

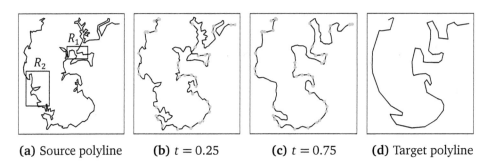

(a) Source polyline   (b) $t = 0.25$ (c) $t = 0.75$ (d) Target polyline

Figure 5.11: Case study on real-world data.

Chapter 6

Choosing the Right Data Structures for Solving Spatial Problems

Detecting corresponding objects, which represent the same real-world entity, from two different spatial datasets has drawn a lot of attention in map generalization [e.g., Nöl+08; PWH16; DP15] and data conflation [e.g., ZM08; Mas06; TLJ14; Rui+11]. However, corresponding objects may have different coordinates because of many reasons. For example, measurements introduce errors, and different organizations may use their own approaches to produce spatial datasets [Bee+05]. An important criteria of determining corresponding objects is to investigate if they have close positions. For example, Beeri et al. [Bee+05] assumed that the locations of objects are given as points and required that corresponding objects should have a distance smaller than a threshold. Based on the work of Beeri et al. [Bee+05], Safra et al. [Saf+13] managed to match road networks. Volz [Vol06] matched street data starting from so-called *seed nodes*. Each pair of their seed nodes should be within a distance of 30 meters. We model the problem of looking for *close* points as follows. For a given set of points, we want to find all the pairs of close points. We consider two points to be close if they lie within a square of a pre-specified side length, say, ε. In other words, points p and q are close if we have distance $L_\infty(p,q) = \max(\Delta x, \Delta y) \le \varepsilon$, where $\Delta x = |p_x - q_x|$ and $\Delta y = |p_y - q_y|$ are the differences of x- and y-coordinates, respectively (see Figure 6.1).

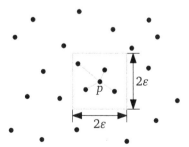

Figure 6.1: For point p, the four linked points are its close points. These close points lie in the square with side length 2ε centered at p.

In order to solve the problem efficiently, we have implemented and tested some ad-hoc solutions, including using different algorithms and different data structures. During this process, we have made a number of observations in terms of running time and memory consumption, cost by the different solutions. We think that it is worth to share our observations with the GIS community. That is to say, the ultimate goal of this chapter is not to identify the algorithm that performs the best for the problem at hand. Rather, we want to address the issues that we had during implementing and testing; we want to discuss the lessons we learned.

A brute-force approach for finding all pairs of close points requires $\Theta(n^2)$ time, where n is the number of points. This running time is worst-case optimal since the size of the output can be $\Theta(n^2)$ if side length ε is sufficiently large. Typically, however, the size of the output is small. Hence, it is desirable to use algorithms whose running time do not only depend on the size of the input (n, the number of points), but also depend on the size of the output, that is, the number of pairs of close points. Such an algorithm is called *output-sensitive*. Note that our problem is different from Saalfeld [Saa88]. For a given point on one map, they wanted to find the single nearest point in another map, which can be accomplished in $O(n \log n)$ time [SH75].

We consider three obvious output-sensitive algorithms: A sweep-line (SL) algorithm, an algorithm based on the Delaunay triangulation (DT), and a hashing-like approach that uses a grid. The sweep-line algorithm runs in $O(k + n \log n)$ worst-case time, where k is the number of pairs of close points, i.e., the size of output. The same running time holds for the algorithm based on the Delaunay triangulation under the assumption that the input points are randomly and independently distributed in a unit square. The definition of this distribution will be shown in Section 6.1. Under the same assumption regarding the distribution of the input, the grid-based algorithm runs in $O(k + n)$ time, which is the most efficient. We sketch the three algorithms in Section 6.1. We have implemented them, and we have compared their performances on random data and real-world data (see Section 6.2). We conclude this chapter in Section 6.3.

We remark that we focus on methods that can be implemented easily. For this reason, we have not included a method that uses two-dimensional range trees [e.g., Ben+77; Lue78; LW80], which is a two-level data structure based on balanced binary search tree (BBST); see Cormen et al. [Cor+09, Chapter 13]. The method works as follows. It inserts all n input points into a range tree. For each point p, it queries the tree with a range of size $2\varepsilon \times 2\varepsilon$ centered at p. The running time of that method is $O(k + n \log^2 n)$, the memory consumption is $O(n \log n)$; see Bentley et al. [Ben+77]. Furthermore, the running time can be improved to $O(k + n \log n)$ by using the fractional cascading [Ber+08, Chapter 5], but we would need additional implementation effort.

6.1 Algorithms

In the following, we sketch the three algorithms. We denote the set of input points by $P = \{p_1, p_2, \ldots, p_n\}$, where point p_i has coordinates (x_i, y_i). While the algorithms work for any input, our running-time analyses will assume that the input points are uniformly and independently distributed (u.i.d.) in the unit square $[0, 1] \times [0, 1]$. We do not record the pairs of close points but just count them, thus we need little extra memory for recording the output.

6.1.1 The Sweep-Line Algorithm

The SL paradigm is a common tool in computational geometry [Ber+08, Chapter 2]. Shamos and Hoey [SH76] developed this algorithm to determine if two polygons intersect. In their case, the SL algorithm runs in $O(n' \log n')$ time, where n' is the total number of the edges of the polygons. Bentley and Ottmann [BO79] extended the SL algorithm so that they could report all the intersections. This extension increases the running time to $O(k' + n' \log n')$, where k' is the number of intersections. Intuitively, the SL algorithm uses a line to sweep the plane, then the line stops at certain events and changes its internal status (see Figure 6.2). The SL algorithm usually employs two data structures: the *event queue* and the *status*. For our problem of searching for close points, we sweep a horizontal line from top to bottom. Our sweep line $l : y = y_l$ stops at the y-coordinates in set $\{y_i, y_i - \varepsilon \mid i = 1, 2, \ldots, n\}$. We store these coordinates (together with references to the corresponding points) in the event queue in decreasing order. The status contains all points in a horizontal strip of height ε bounded by lines l and $l_\varepsilon : y = y_l + \varepsilon$. We store the points according to their x-coordinates using a BBST in increasing order. To implement the event queue, it suffices to sort the $2n$ y-coordinates and store the sorted coordinates in an array.

We have only two types of events: *enter* and *leave*. Point p_i enters the status when the sweep line hits it, that is, when $y_l = y_i$. At the same time, we report each pair (p_i, p_j), where p_j is a point in the status with $x_i - \varepsilon \leq x_j \leq x_i + \varepsilon$. Such a *points-in-interval* query is supported by BBSTs. The query takes $O(k_i + \log n)$ time, where k_i is the number of points that are reported for p_i. Point p_i leaves the status when the sweep line reaches the y-coordinate $y_i - \varepsilon$. Summing up the running time for each point yields a total running time of $O(k + n \log n)$, where k is the size of the output, that is, the number of close-point pairs. The memory consumption of the SL algorithm is $O(n)$.

The C# implementation of BBST is *SortedDictionary* (SD), which does not offer a specific points-in-interval query. Instead, SD offers method *where*, which takes an arbitrary predicate as argument and returns all currently stored objects that fulfill the predicate, but this method takes linear time. The linear time is not a problem as long as side length ε is so small that the strip, with height ε and above the sweep line, never contains many points. In the worst case, however, the running time

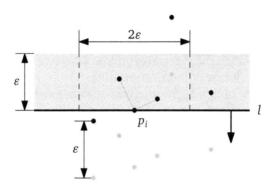

Figure 6.2: An illustration of our SL algorithm. The sweep line l is moving from top to bottom. The black points are the data that we are looking for close points. The gray points are the references to the corresponding black points. The gray strip represents the status which is implemented by a BBST. The black points in the status are the potential close points. When the sweep line hits a black point, we search for close points in the status and then enter the black point into the status; when the sweep line hits a gray point, we remove the corresponding black point from the status. In this example, the sweep line hits point $p_i = (x_i, y_i)$. It is sufficient to search in the interval $[x_i - \varepsilon, x_i + \varepsilon]$ of the status. As a result, we find two close points, which are linked to p_i.

becomes quadratic even if there is no pair of close points at all. Luckily, the BBST implementations *SortedSet* (SS) from .NET Framework 4.0 and *TreeSet* (TS) from library C5 both support the points-in-interval query. Library C5 is an open-source C# data structure from Kokholm and Sestoft [KS06]. In addition, *TreeSet* of language Java also supports the points-in-interval query.

6.1.2 The Delaunay-Triangulation-Based Algorithm

The DT is a useful tool for partitioning the plane such that spatially close points are connected by the edges of the DT. For example, it is well-known that the line segment between any point and its closest neighbor is an edge of the DT. Given the DT, we go through the points and start a modified *breadth-first search* (BFS) from each of them [e.g., MD10; RKW13]. BFS is a well-known graph traversal algorithm [Cor+09, chapter 22]. For input point p, our BFS considers every point $q \neq p$ with $L_\infty(p, q) \leq (1 + \sqrt{2})\varepsilon/2$. We say that $r_1 = (1 + \sqrt{2})\varepsilon/2 \approx 1.2\varepsilon$ is the *radius* of our BFS. The reason for using r_1 is simply that a radius of ε is not sufficient; we may, in rare cases, oversee some pairs of close points. In Figure 6.3, for an instance, if we set $\varepsilon = 0.003$, then p and q are a pair of close points. But we cannot find this pair if we only check points within a distance of ε because there is at least one point lying outside the square in every path from p to q or from q to p. It is not hard to see that r_1 is necessary. Unfortunately, we cannot prove it. We conjecture that r_1 is indeed sufficient. This conjecture is supported by our experiments where we found all pairs of close points by using radius r_1.

Here, we show that radius $r = \left(\sqrt{2} + \sqrt{14}\right)\varepsilon/4 \approx 1.3\varepsilon$ is sufficient. According to Xia [Xia13], the DT contains, for any two input points p and q, a path of length less than $2|pq|$ connecting p and q. We observe that such a path is contained in ellipse E_{pq}, which uses foci p and q and major axis $2|pq|$. We are interested in the maximum x- or y-coordinate of E_{pq} for a fixed point p (say $p = (0,0)$) and any point q of L_∞-distance at most ε. One can show that the maximum x-coordinate of E_{pq} is maximized if $q = (\varepsilon, \varepsilon)$; see Figure 6.4a. In this case, the maximum x-coordinate of E_{pq} is $\left(\sqrt{2} + \sqrt{14}\right)\varepsilon/4$, which is the value we use for r. This can be seen by some elementary geometry (see Figure 6.4b). We move p to $(-1/2, 0)$ and q to $(1/2, 0)$. Then E_{pq} is described by equation $3x^2 + 4y^2 = 3$. Tangent T, with slope 1, can be described by equation $y = x - \sqrt{7}/2$. The distance from point p to tangent T is $\left(\sqrt{2} + \sqrt{14}\right)\varepsilon/4$. In the original coordinate system (see Figure 6.4a), this tangent corresponds to the vertical line $x = \left(\sqrt{2} + \sqrt{14}\right)\varepsilon/4$. However, in our experiment, we use radius $r_2 = \left(1 + \sqrt{7}\right)\varepsilon/2 \approx 1.8\varepsilon$ ($r_2 > r_1$) because we made a mistake in an earlier version of the derivation. Using radius r_2 will not influence our main result because the DT-based algorithm is slower than other algorithms even when we use radius r_1.

Constructing the DT takes $O(n \log n)$ time and $O(n)$ memory [Lea92]. Actually, under our assumption concerning the input distribution, the DT can be constructed in linear time [Buc09], but we will not exploit this here. Assuming that the points are u.i.d. in the unit square, the running time of the DT-based algorithm is in $O(k + n \log n)$. The memory consumption of the DT-based algorithm is in $O(n)$.

6.1.3   The Grid-Based Algorithm

The third algorithm that we consider overlays the input points with a regular rectangular grid. It makes sense to set the side length σ of the grid cells to at least ε (see Figure 6.5). Then, for each input point p, it suffices to check the points in the cell containing p and in the eight neighboring cells. To represent the grid, we use a two-dimensional array of size $(y_{max} - y_{min})/\sigma \times (x_{max} - x_{min})/\sigma$, where x_{max} denotes the maximum x-coordinate among all the points; x_{min}, y_{max}, and y_{min} are defined analogously to x_{max}. Each entry of the grid has a reference to a list (LinkedList in C#) that stores the points in the corresponding cell. In order to ensure a memory consumption of $O(n)$, we set σ to $\max(\varepsilon, \sqrt{c/n})$, where c is the expected number of points in each entry of the grid. This setting is similar to Bentley et al. [BWY80], where they used the grid-based algorithm to find the closest point.

For each of the input points, we compute the two indices of the cell containing that point. This computation includes (i) dividing the coordinates of p by σ and (ii) applying the floor function. If we assume that the input is u.i.d. in the unit square, the expected number of point pairs we check in total is $O(\varepsilon^2 n^2) = O(k)$, and the grid-based algorithm runs in $O(k + n)$ time.

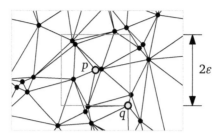

Figure 6.3: An instance of the DT. The line segments between the points are the edges of the DT. The side length of the square is $2\varepsilon = 0.006$; $p = (0.169134, 0.264491)$ and $q = (0.171957, 0.261496)$, thus $|\Delta x_{pq}| = 0.002823$ and $|\Delta y_{pq}| = 0.002995$.

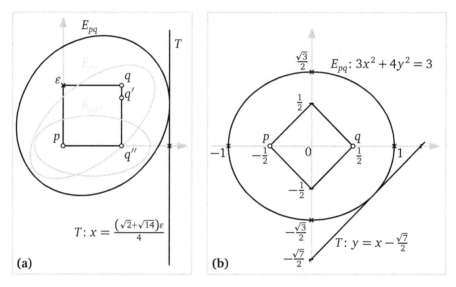

Figure 6.4: Among all points of L_∞-distance at most ε from p, the point $q = (\varepsilon, \varepsilon)$ gives rise to an ellipse E_{pq} whose right vertical tangent T has maximum x-coordinate (a). For deriving the equation of T more easily, we transform p, q, E_{pq}, and T into the coordinate system of (b).

6.2 Case Study

We implemented the three algorithms in C# (using the .NET Framework 4.0). We ran our experiments under Windows 7 on a 3.3 GHz dual core CPU with 8 GB RAM. We measured time and memory consumption by using the built-in C# methods System.Environment.TickCount and GC.GetTotalMemory(true). For the DT, we took advantage of an implementation available in ArcGIS Engine 10.1. As we did not find a way to measure the memory consumption of the DT directly, we saved the files for the DT, i.e., files in .adf format from ArcGIS Engine 10.1 (an instance of the DT consists of 10 files), to the hard disk and measured the sum of the 10 files' sizes.

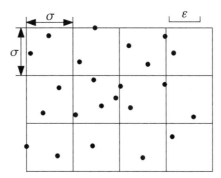

Figure 6.5: Overlaying the points with a grid.

We show the results obtained by the DT-based algorithm with both radii r_1 and r_2; we use $DT\ r_1$ and $DT\ r_2$ to denote the respective total running times. We use *DT total* to denote the memory consumption of the DT-based algorithm and use *DT constr.* to denote the time or memory consumption of the DT construction; these values are independent of the radius. Recall that we denote SortedDictionary from C# by SD, SortedSet from C# by SS, and TreeSet from C5 by TS.

We tested the three algorithms on both random data and real-world data. There were ten sets of points for each type of data. We used N to denote the number of points in the set that had most points among the ten sets. We considered two different ways to set side length ε. One way was that we set ε to a certain value, say ε_0, independent of the instance size. This means that the size of the output, $k = \Theta(\varepsilon^2 n^2)$, grows quadratically. The other way was to set $\varepsilon = \varepsilon_0 \sqrt{N/n}$, which means that ε decreases from $\varepsilon_0 \sqrt{N/n}$ to ε_0 and k grows linearly.

6.2.1 Case Study on Random Data

We randomly generated ten point sets u.i.d. in the unit square. The sizes of the point sets range from 20,000 to 200,000 with steps of size 20,000 (see for example Figure 6.6). According to our definition, $N = 200,000$. We set $\varepsilon_0 = 0.003$. For the grid-based algorithm, we set side length $\sigma = \varepsilon_0 \sqrt{N/n}$.

Time Consumption

In the experiment with $\varepsilon = \varepsilon_0$ (see Figure 6.7), the quadratic size of the output dominates the actual time consumption of the DT-based algorithm (see Figure 6.7a). The same holds for the C# SortedDictionary implementation of the SL algorithm (see Figure 6.7a). The implementations of C# SortedSet and C5 TreeSet both perform in a linearithmic way, and the grid-based algorithm performs linearly (see Figure 6.7b). In the three cases, the actual time consumption is dominated by the term that depends on the size of input, n.

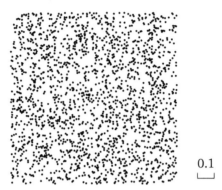

0.1

Figure 6.6: As it is difficult to present too many points. we randomly select about 10%, 2046, of the points from our dataset with 20,000 points u.i.d. in the unit square.

In the experiment with $\varepsilon = \varepsilon_0 \sqrt{N/n}$ (see Figure 6.8), the DT-based algorithm, however, now shows a (near-)linear time consumption (see Figure 6.8a). Still, it is much slower than the other four implementations. Interestingly, the implementation based on C# SortedDictionary still shows a quadratic behavior (see Figure 6.8a). This is due to the fact that the height-ε strip above the sweep line contains an expected linear number of points ($n\varepsilon$), which are traversed by the *where* method of the SortedDictionary data structure. According to Figure 6.8b, the C# SortedSet, C5 TreeSet, and the grid-based implementations perform similarly as in the experiment with $\varepsilon = \varepsilon_0$. In both experiments, the simple grid-based algorithm is by far the fastest (by a factor of roughly 7); see Figures 6.7b and 6.8b.

We also observed that, in both experiments, the time of computing the DT was about the same as the running times of the two SL implementations (see Figures 6.7b and 6.8b). Indeed, the running time of computing the DT is also $O(n \log n)$; see Section 6.1.2. In addition, The DT-based algorithm with radius r_1 is faster than that with radius r_2 by a factor of 2.

Output Size and Memory Consumption

The curves of the output size perform as expected (see Figure 6.9). The output size grows in a quadratic way when we set $\varepsilon = \varepsilon_0$ and grows linearly when we set $\varepsilon = \varepsilon_0 \sqrt{N/n}$ (see Figure 6.9a). As said before, we did not record the pairs of close points but just counted the number of pairs, we basically did not need any extra memory for the output. Therefore, the two experiments with different values of side length ε need the same amount of memory. Figure 6.9b shows that the memory consumption of all our methods grows linearly. Among the five implementations, the grid-based algorithm uses the least amount of memory, which is less than the DT-based algorithm by a factor of 1.2. We can also see that the C# SortedSet BBST needs the least memory to implement the SL algorithm; about 10% less than the C5 TreeSet implementation.

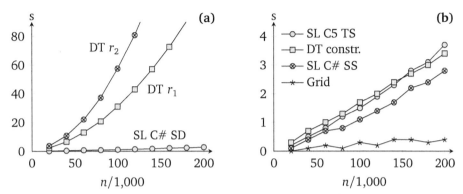

Figure 6.7: Time consumption of the algorithms when $\varepsilon = \varepsilon_0$. The DT-based algorithm took 109 s with radius r_1 ("DT r_1") and 217 s with radius r_2 ("DT r_2") for $n = 200,000$.

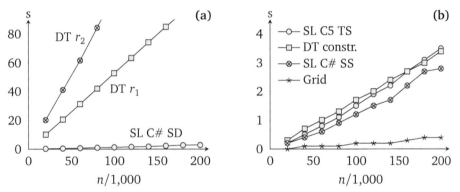

Figure 6.8: Time consumption of the algorithms when $\varepsilon = \varepsilon_0 \sqrt{N/n}$. The DT-based algorithm took 106 s with radius r_1 ("DT r_1") and 216 s with radius r_2 ("DT r_2") for $n = 200,000$.

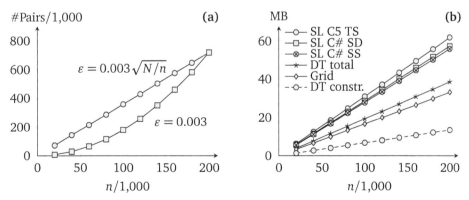

Figure 6.9: Output size and memory consumption of the algorithms for the random data.

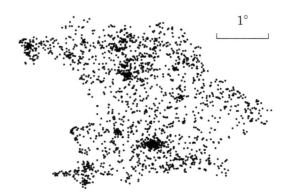

Figure 6.10: The point data of Bavaria. There are originally 277,034 points. We present about 1%, 2,722, of the points in this figure. The presented points are selected randomly.

6.2.2 Case Study on Real-World Data

We use a set P of 277,034 points from OpenStreetMap that represent bus stops, milestones, hotels, post boxes, etc. in the state of Bavaria, Germany (see Figure 6.10). After deleting duplicates, we had $N_0 = 276,992$ points left. We computed the *average distance* as

$$d_{\text{avg}} = \sqrt{(x_{\text{max}} - x_{\text{min}}) \cdot (y_{\text{max}} - y_{\text{min}})/N_0},$$

where coordinates x_{max}, x_{min}, y_{max}, and y_{min} are defined as in Section 6.1.3. According to our data, $x_{\text{max}} = 13.846676°$, $x_{\text{min}} = 8.974805°$, $y_{\text{max}} = 50.555617°$, and $y_{\text{min}} = 47.270111°$. Therefore, we have $d_{\text{avg}} = 0.007602°$.

We perturbed the points according to a Gaussian distribution. For each point, we generated a pair of normally distributed numbers X and Y by the Box-Muller transform [see BM58]. Then we set the new coordinates as

$$\left. \begin{array}{l} x_i' = x_i + \delta \cdot X_i \\ y_i' = y_i + \delta \cdot Y_i \end{array} \right\},$$

where x_i and y_i are the original coordinates, and standard deviation $\delta = d_{\text{avg}}/6 = 0.001267°$. After perturbing, we had two points sets, i.e., the original set P and a perturbed set P', which models that we have two point sets from different sources. Now, we try to find the corresponding points. In order to extract from P ten datasets of different sizes, i.e., datasets $P_1, P_2, \ldots, P_{10}$, we selected for P_j each point in P with probability $j/10$. Hence, datasets $|P_j| \approx |P| \cdot j/10$ and $|P_{10}| = |P|$.

For $j = 1, 2, \ldots, 10$, let dataset $\bar{P}_j = P_j \cup P_j'$, where P_j' is the set of perturbed points obtained from the points in P_j. These are the sets we used in our experiments (see Figures 6.11, 6.12, and 6.13).

We set $\varepsilon_0 = \delta$. Because of the perturbation, we have $N = 2 \cdot 276{,}992 = 553{,}984$. For the grid-based algorithm, setting σ to $\varepsilon_0 \sqrt{N/n}$ would yield too many grid cells (18 times the number of points). We would need a lot of memory to record these cells and a lot of time to initialize the LinkedList entries. To avoid this problem, we set σ to $\frac{d_{avg}}{\sqrt{2}} \sqrt{N/n}$. By this setting, the number of grid cells is roughly the same as the number of points.

Time Consumption

We got similar results as in Section 6.2.1. An interesting difference is that although the grid-based algorithm is still the fastest, the factor decreases to roughly 2 (see Figure 6.11b). There are two reasons. One is that the ratio of σ to ε has changed. When $n = N$, the ratio is 1 for the case study on random data, while it is $3\sqrt{2}$ for the case study on real-world data. This increasing leads the grid-based algorithm to check more points in the case study on real-world data. The other reason is that the size of the real-world output dominates the running time a bit more. There are on average 10.8 close points for one point in the case study on real-world data when $N = 553{,}984$ and $\varepsilon = \delta$, while the number is 7.2 for the case study on random data when $N = 200{,}000$ and $\varepsilon = 0.003$. Also note that now the construction time of the DT is less than the running time of the two implementations of the SL algorithm (e.g., comparing Figures 6.7b and 6.11b). The DT-based algorithm with radius r_1 is faster than that with radius r_2 by a factor of roughly 3 (see Figures 6.11a and 6.12a).

Output Size and Memory Consumption

Also, the curves of the output size perform as expected (see Figure 6.13a). For the grid-based algorithm, when we try to achieve that there are roughly the same numbers of entries and points, we need more memory compared to the case study on random data (comparing Figures 6.9b and 6.13b). However, the grid-based algorithm still uses less memory than the DT-based algorithm by a factor of 1.1, and it still uses less memory than the SL implementations by a factor of 1.6; see Figure 6.13b.

6.3 Concluding Remarks

Although the grid-based algorithm was the clear winner of our comparison, we were more interested in the results of the three implementations of the SL algorithm. The SL paradigm can be used to solve many problems, e.g., computing the Voronoi diagram [For87], for which the grid approach would not work. When implementing the SL algorithm, it was tempting to use the data structures available in C# (for example, the method *where* of SortedDictionary), but we have seen that it is worth to read the fine print.

Even from the slowest algorithm, based on the DT, we have learned something. By comparison with the other implementations, we noticed that the radius-ε BFS missed a few pairs of close points in the case study on random data (just 5 out of the 718,775 pairs of close points that were reported in the 200,000-point instance for $\varepsilon = 0.003$). Then we conjectured that a radius of $(1+\sqrt{2})\varepsilon/2 \approx 1.2\varepsilon$ is sufficient, which was supported by our experiments where we found all pairs of close points. We also proved that a radius of $(\sqrt{2} + \sqrt{14})\varepsilon/4 \approx 1.3\varepsilon$ is sufficient. Of course, enlarging the radius slowed down the method. It turned out that, however, a radius of $(1 + \sqrt{2})\varepsilon/2$ is sometimes necessary. An interesting future work is to prove that, in the DT-based algorithm, radius $(1 + \sqrt{2})\varepsilon/2$ is sufficient for finding all the pairs of close points.

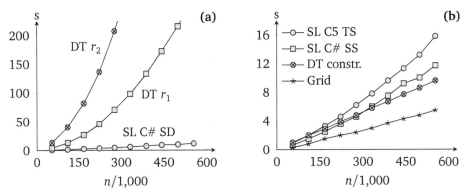

Figure 6.11: Time consumption of the algorithms when $\varepsilon = \delta$. The DT-based algorithm took 262 s with radius r_1 ("DT r_1") and 784 s with radius r_2 ("DT r_2") for $n = 553,984$. The axes and the notations are as in Figure 6.7.

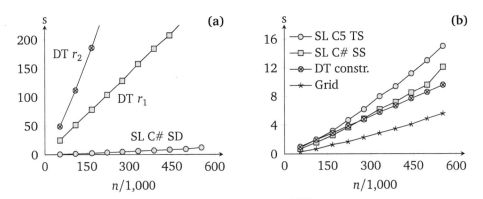

Figure 6.12: Time consumption of the algorithms when $\varepsilon = \delta\sqrt{N/n}$. The DT-based algorithm took 267 s with radius r_1 ("DT r_1") and 810 s with radius r_2 ("DT r_2") for $n = 553,984$.

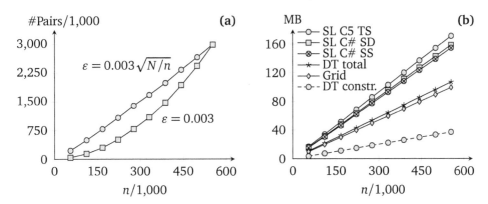

Figure 6.13: Output size and memory consumption of the algorithms for the real-world data.

Chapter 7

Conclusions and Open Problems

7.1 Conclusions

In this thesis, we have studied four topics of continuous map generalization. These topics include area aggregation, morphing between administrative boundaries, building generalization, and defining trajectories for morphing polylines. Although we focus on providing smooth transitions, the intermediate-scale results of the four methods may be used as valid maps. Also, we have presented some lessons that we learned from implementing our algorithms. In order to achieve continuous map generalization of high quality, we have integrated optimization into our methods. We made most of the drawings in this thesis using *Ipe* [see Sch95]. When we were making drawings, we considered the suggestions of colors from *ColorBrewer* [see HB03; BHH03].

A number of methods have been developed for continuous map generalization. However, as maps are complicated, we need to develop more methods in order to fully automate continuous map generalization. Besides, an urgent issue is to unify the methods. Currently, each of our methods deals with only one type of feature, i.e., land-cover areas, buildings, or administrative boundaries. A map usually contains many kinds of features. It would be interesting to work on a complete map, where we would need to care about the relations between different kinds of features. For example, depending on the situations, we may use streets to confine the growing of buildings to built-up areas, or we may cover the streets with built-up areas because we want to aggregate several blocks into one. Furthermore, we should make rules for producing source maps to allow these maps to be generalized more easily.

The main goal of continuous map generalization is to provide users with better zoom experience. Hence, more usability tests are needed to see if the results of continuous map generalization are indeed better than other zoom strategies. We planed to compare our work about building generalization (see Chapter 4) with the results of *progressive block graying* [see TD17]. As they and we have obtained results based on different strategies, it is possible (and necessary) to make a comparison based on some usability test. To this end, we should design some tasks (e.g., pointing out the position of a building during zooming out), and then ask participants to complete these tasks [e.g., MN07]. Then we can compare the time and the accuracies of users' working on the tasks. Moreover, Šuba et al. [Šub+16] have already made a plan for testing vario-scale maps, which is related to our research.

It is important to generate intermediate-scale results that have simple relations among each other. These simple relations often result in small extra storage and real-time visualization. Our intermediate-scale maps of area aggregation (see Chapter 2) have simple relations. These maps can be stored easily using the generalized area partitioning tree (GAP-tree). In order to display our morphing between two sets of administrative boundaries, we only need to store the two datasets and a set of relations between the two datasets. When users are zooming, we only need to interpolate linearly between the two sets of administrative boundaries on the fly[7]. Our intermediate-scale maps of buildings (see Chapter 4), however, have no simple relations. Currently, we clumsily store many intermediate-scale maps and then transfer all these maps to users when they are zooming. This strategy may cause time lags. We should either improve our method of generating intermediate-scale maps or find a way to construct simple relations between our current intermediate-scale maps.

We want to make our prototype more easily accessible for other scientists. Although our prototype is open access on GitHub[8], one needs to install and configure many libraries in order to run the prototype on their own computers. We wish to put our prototype on a server and allow other scientists to access our prototype through a website software as a service. The computation should be on the server, while the users can input their own data and get the output. Also, We would like to make our prototype more user-friendly.

7.2 Open Problems

In Chapter 2, we have shown how to compute optimal aggregation sequences for land-cover maps. We tried solving this problem by a greedy algorithm, the A* algorithm, and a method based on integer linear programming. For the A* algorithm, we have a good estimation for the cost of type change, which helps a lot to reduce the search space, but our estimation for the cost of shape (compactness or edge length) is rather poor. The ILP-based algorithm, on the other hand, could not even find *feasible* solutions for some of our test instances. We have the following open problems.

Open Problem 1. How to find a better estimation for the cost of shape (compactness or edge length)?

Open Problem 2. Do we need to consider other aspects in our cost function? How to set weights to different kinds of aspects?

Open Problem 3. Is there an ILP formulation that can be solved faster than ours?

---

[7]   For some examples, see www1.pub.informatik.uni-wuerzburg.de/pub/data/agile2016/.
[8]   See https://github.com/IGNF/ContinuousGeneralisation.

In Chapter 3, we have continuously generalized county boundaries to provincial boundaries by morphing. Recall that there are more boundaries on the county map. In order to morph a county boundary that is not at the same time a provincial boundary, we generate the corresponding boundary based on compatible triangulations. We observed that some of the boundaries that we generated are heavily distorted. These distortions lead us to the following open problems.

Open Problem 4. How much can we reduce the distortion if we use common chords as many as possible when constructing compatible triangulations?

Open Problem 5. Can we efficiently minimize the distortion over all generated boundaries?

Open Problem 6. How to properly evaluate our continuous generalization of administrative boundaries?

In Chapter 4, we continuously generalized buildings to built-up areas by aggregating and growing. We managed to produce a sequence of maps in which we grew and simplified the buildings. We compared the numbers of buildings with the numbers implied by the law of Töpfer and Pillewizer [TP66]. Although this law has been criticized by Jiang [Jia15], who proposed calculating the numbers of objects according to the fractal nature of maps, there is no generally accepted formula for computing the numbers so far. Therefore, the following questions remain open.

Open Problem 7. For a given map and a scale, how many buildings should be kept after generalization?

Open Problem 8. Again, for a given map and a scale, how much total area of buildings should be kept after generalization? What about the total number of edges?

Open Problem 9. How to avoid the lengthy buildings generated by our method?

Open Problem 10. How to design a meaningful user study to evaluate our and other approaches to continuous building generalization?

In Chapter 5, we have introduced a method for morphing polylines that tries to change angles and edge lengths linearly over time. Our approach is based on least-squares adjustment. The approach can handle both hard and soft constraints. Our first results are promising. Still, there are open problems.

Open Problem 11. How can we ensure that our LSA-based method always converges to a good solution?

Open Problem 12. Do we have better models for the changes of angles and edge lengths, instead of using linear functions?

Open Problem 13. How to avoid self-intersections of a polyline during a morph? How to avoid a polyline intersecting other polylines?

In Chapter 6, we have compared three methods for finding close-point pairs, i.e., a sweep-line algorithm, an algorithm based on the Delaunay triangulation, and a grid-based algorithm. The grid-based algorithm was the clear winner of our comparison. However, the sweep-line paradigm can be used to solve many problems, e.g., computing the Voronoi diagram [For87]. The following questions remain open.

Open Problem 14. What is the smallest radius such that the algorithm based on Delaunay triangulation finds *all* pairs of close points?

Open Problem 15. Is the grid-based algorithm faster than other algorithms, including those not mentioned in the chapter, in finding close edges or close polygons?

Open Problem 16. Will the grid-based algorithm be the winner when we extend the three methods to higher dimensions?

Bibliography

[Ark+91]   Arkin, E. M., Chew, L. P., Huttenlocher, D. P., Kedem, K., and Mitchell, J. S. B. An efficiently computable metric for comparing polygonal shapes. In: *IEEE Transactions on Pattern Analysis and Machine Intelligence* 13.3 (1991), pp. 209–216. DOI: 10.1109/34.75509 [see p. 87].

[ASS93]   Aronov, B., Seidel, R., and Souvaine, D. L. On compatible triangulations of simple polygons. In: *Computational Geometry* 3 (1993), pp. 27–35. DOI: 10.1016/0925-7721(93)90028-5 [see pp. 53, 54, 60].

[BSW97]   Babikov, M., Souvaine, D. L., and Wenger, R. Constructing piecewise linear homeomorphisms of polygons with holes. In: *Proc. 9th Canadian Conference on Computational Geometry (CCCG)*. 1997, pp. 6–10. URL: http://www.cccg.ca/proceedings/1997/cccg1997.pdf [see p. 66].

[Bee+05]   Beeri, C., Doytsher, Y., Kanza, Y., Safra, E., and Sagiv, Y. Finding corresponding objects when integrating several geo-spatial datasets. In: *Proc. 13th Annual ACM International Workshop on Geographic Information Systems*. 2005, pp. 87–96. DOI: 10/dhfprh [see p. 97].

[BO79]   Bentley, J. L. and Ottmann, T. A. Algorithms for reporting and counting geometric intersections. In: *IEEE Transactions on Computers* C-28.9 (1979), pp. 643–647. DOI: 10.1109/TC.1979.1675432 [see p. 99].

[Ben+77]   Bentley, J. L., Shamos, M. I., Bentley, J. L., and Shamos, M. I. A problem in multivariate statistics: Algorithm, data structure, and applications. In: *Proc. 15th Allerton Conference on Communication, Control, and Computing*. 1977, pp. 193–201. URL: http://www.dtic.mil/docs/citations/ADA055818 [see p. 98].

[BWY80]   Bentley, J. L., Weide, B. W., and Yao, A. C. Optimal expected-time algorithms for closest point problems. In: *ACM Transactions on Mathematical Software* 6.4 (1980), pp. 563–580. DOI: 10.1145/355921.355927 [see p. 101].

[Ber05]   Bereg, S. An approximate morphing between polylines. In: *International Journal of Computational Geometry & Applications* 15.2 (2005), pp. 193–208. DOI: 10.1142/S0218195905001658 [see pp. 59, 93].

[Ber+08]   de Berg, M., Cheong, O., van Kreveld, M., and Overmars, M. *Computational Geometry: Algorithms and Applications*. 3rd ed. Springer-Verlag, 2008. DOI: 10.1007/978-3-662-03427-9 [see pp. 55, 98, 99].

[Bof00]   Boffet, A. Creating urban information for cartographic generalisation.
            In: *Proc. 9th International Symposium on Spatial Data Handling (SDH),
            Advances in GIS Research III*. Ed. by P. Forer, A. Yeh, and J. He. Lec-
            ture Notes in Geoinformation and Cartography. 2000. URL: http://
            recherche.ign.fr/labos/util_basilic/publicDownload.php?id=3284
            [see p. 79].

[BM58]   Box, G. E. P. and Muller, M. E. A note on the generation of random
            normal deviates. In: *The Annals of Mathematical Statistics* 29.2 (1958),
            pp. 610–611. DOI: 10.1214/aoms/1177706645 [see p. 106].

[BHM77]   Bradley, S. P., Hax, A. C., and Magnanti, T. L. *Applied Mathematical
            Programming*. Addison-Wesley Publishing Company, 1977. URL: http:
            //web.mit.edu/15.053/www/AMP.htm [see p. 29].

[BB07]   Brewer, C. A. and Buttenfield, B. P. Framing guidelines for multi-scale
            map design using databases at multiple resolutions. In: *Cartography
            and Geographic Information Science* 34.1 (2007), pp. 3–15. DOI: 10/
            dm5jj6 [see p. 12].

[BHH03]   Brewer, C. A., Hatchard, G. W., and Harrower, M. A. Colorbrewer in
            print: A catalog of color schemes for maps. In: *Cartography and Geo-
            graphic Information Science* 30.1 (2003), pp. 5–32. DOI: 10/df3png
            [see p. 111].

[Bro+15]   Bronstein, I. N., Semendjajew, K. A., Musiol, G., and Mühlig, H. *Hand-
            book of Mathematics*. 6th ed. Springer-Verlag Berlin Heidelberg, 2015.
            DOI: 10.1007/978-3-662-46221-8 [see p. 57].

[Buc09]   Buchin, K. Constructing Delaunay triangulations along space-filling cur-
            ves. In: *Proc. 17th Annual European Symposium on Algorithms (ESA)*.
            Ed. by A. Fiat and P. Sanders. Vol. 5757. Lecture Notes in Computer
            Science. 2009, pp. 119–130. DOI: 10/bt8qfk [see p. 101].

[BMS11]   Buchin, K., Meulemans, W., and Speckmann, B. A new method for sub-
            division simplification with applications to urban-area generalization.
            In: *Proc. 19th ACM SIGSPATIAL International Conference on Advances in
            Geographic Information Systems (ACMGIS)*. Ed. by I. F. Cruz, D. Agrawal,
            C. S. Jensen, E. Ofek, and E. Tanin. 2011, pp. 261–270. DOI: 10.1145/
            2093973.2094009 [see p. 68].

[Bur05]   Burghardt, D. Controlled line smoothing by snakes. In: *GeoInformatica*
            9.3 (2005), pp. 237–252. DOI: 10/dfjwz5 [see p. 3].

[Cec03]   Cecconi, A. Integration of cartographic generalization and multi-scale
            databases for enhanced web mapping. PhD thesis. Universität Zürich,
            Switzerland, 2003. DOI: 10/c5kd [see pp. 2, 51, 85].

[CC96]   Chan, W. and Chin, F. Approximation of polygonal curves with min-
            imum number of line segments or minimum error. In: *International
            Journal of Computational Geometry & Applications* 06.01 (1996), pp.
            59–77. DOI: 10.1142/S0218195996000058 [see p. 78].

[CM08]   Chaudhry, O. and Mackaness, W. A. Automatic identification of urban
            settlement boundaries for multiple representation databases. In: *Com-
            puters, Environment and Urban Systems* 32.2 (2008), pp. 95–109. DOI:
            10.1016/j.compenvurbsys.2007.09.001 [see pp. 68, 73, 76, 77, 84].

[Cha+10]   Chazal, F., Lieutier, A., Rossignac, J., and Whited, B. Ball-map: Home-
            omorphism between compatible surfaces. In: *International Journal of
            Computational Geometry & Applications* 20.3 (2010), pp. 285–306. DOI:
            10/dnrwhn [see p. 2].

[CL06]   Cheng, T. and Li, Z. Toward quantitative measures for the semantic
            quality of polygon generalization. In: *Cartographica* 41.2 (2006), pp.
            487–499. DOI: 10.3138/0172-6733-227U-8155 [see pp. 17, 18].

[CDH14]   Chimani, M., van Dijk, T. C., and Haunert, J.-H. How to eat a graph:
            Computing selection sequences for the continuous generalization of
            road networks. In: *Proc. 22nd ACM SIGSPATIAL International Confer-
            ence on Advances in Geographic Information Systems (ACMGIS)*. 2014,
            pp. 243–252. DOI: 10.1145/2666310.2666414 [see pp. 4, 67].

[CDR03]   Connelly, R., Demaine, E. D., and Rote, G. Straightening polygonal arcs
            and convexifying polygonal cycles. In: *Discrete & Computational Geom-
            etry* 30.2 (2003), pp. 205–239. DOI: 10/cv63dt [see p. 87].

[Cor+09]   Cormen, T. H., Leiserson, C. E., Rivest, R. L., and Stein, C. *Introduction
            to Algorithms*. 3rd ed. The MIT Press, 2009. URL: https://mitpress.mit.
            edu/books/introduction-algorithms-third-edition [see pp. 4, 5, 13, 16,
            49, 98, 100].

[CC00]   Cova, T. J. and Church, R. L. Contiguity constraints for single-region
            site search problems. In: *Geographical Analysis* 32.4 (2000), pp. 306–
            329. DOI: 10.1111/j.1538-4632.2000.tb00430.x [see p. 35].

[DKS08]   Damen, J., van Kreveld, M., and Spaan, B. High quality building gen-
            eralization by extending the morphological operators. In: *Proc. 12th
            ICA Workshop on Generalisation and Multiple Representation (ICAGM)*.
            2008. URL: https://bertspaan.nl/files/building-generalization.pdf
            [see pp. 68, 71].

[Dan+09]   Danciger, J., Devadoss, S. L., Mugno, J., Sheehy, D., and Ward, R. Shape
            deformation in continuous map generalization. In: *GeoInformatica* 13.2
            (2009), pp. 203–221. DOI: 10/d24vxs [see pp. 2, 51, 67].

[DP15]   Deng, M. and Peng, D. Morphing linear features based on their entire
            structures. In: *Transactions in GIS* 19.5 (2015), pp. 653–677. DOI: 10.
            1111/tgis.12111 [see pp. 2, 51, 67, 97].

[Dij59]   Dijkstra, E. W. A note on two problems in connexion with graphs. In: *Numerische Mathematik* 1.1 (1959), pp. 269–271. DOI: 10/dpvk8c [see pp. 5, 16, 23].

[DOH09]   Dilo, A., van Oosterom, P., and Hofman, A. Constrained tGAP for generalization between scales: The case of Dutch topographic data. In: *Computers, Environment and Urban Systems* 33.5 (2009), pp. 388–402. DOI: 10.1016/j.compenvurbsys.2009.07.006 [see pp. 18, 49].

[Diw+11] Diwan, A. A., Ghosh, S. K., Goswami, P. P., and Lingas, A. On joint triangulations of two sets of points in the plane. In: *Computing Research Repository (CoRR)* abs/1102.1235 (2011). URL: http://arxiv.org/abs/1102.1235 [see p. 66].

[DP73]   Douglas, D. H. and Peucker, T. K. Algorithms for the reduction of the number of points required to represent a digitized line or its caricature. In: *Cartographica* 10.2 (1973), pp. 112–122. DOI: 10.3138/fm57-6770-u75u-7727 [see pp. 13, 53, 54, 59, 76].

[DFE01]   Doytsher, Y., Filin, S., and Ezra, E. Transformation of datasets in a linear-based map conflation framework. In: *Surveying and Land Information Systems* 61.3 (2001), pp. 159–169 [see pp. 53, 54, 63, 66].

[Duc+14]   Duchêne, C. et al. Generalisation in practice within national mapping agencies. In: *Abstracting Geographic Information in a Data Rich World: Methodologies and Applications of Map Generalisation*. Ed. by D. Burghardt, C. Duchêne, and W. Mackaness. Lecture Notes in Geoinformation and Cartography. 2014. Chap. 11, pp. 329–391. DOI: 10.1007/978-3-319-00203-3_11 [see p. 1].

[Fan+16]   Fan, H., Yang, B., Zipf, A., and Rousell, A. A polygon-based approach for matching OpenStreetMap road networks with regional transit authority data. In: *International Journal of Geographical Information Science* 30.4 (2016), pp. 748–764. DOI: 10/c5kf [see p. 55].

[For87]   Fortune, S. A sweepline algorithm for voronoi diagrams. In: *Algorithmica* 2.1 (1987), pp. 153–174. DOI: 10.1007/BF01840357 [see pp. 107, 114].

[FE06]   Frank, R. and Ester, M. A quantitative similarity measure for maps. In: *Proc. 12th International Symposium on Spatial Data Handling (SDH)*. Ed. by A. Riedl, W. Kainz, and G. A. Elmes. 2006, pp. 435–450. DOI: 10.1007/3-540-35589-8_28 [see p. 87].

[Fro75]   Frolov, Y. S. Measuring the shape of geographical phenomena: a history of the issue. In: *Soviet Geography* 16.10 (1975), pp. 676–687. DOI: 10.1080/00385417.1975.10640104 [see p. 18].

[Fun+17]   Funke, S., Mendel, T., Miller, A., Storandt, S., and Wiebe, M. Map sim-
            plification with topology constraints: exactly and in practice. In: *Proc.*
            19th Workshop on Algorithm Engineering and Experiments (ALENEX).
            2017, pp. 185–196. DOI: 10/c3s3 [see p. 4].

[FS04]   Fuse, T. and Shimizu, E. Visualizing the landscape of old-time Tokyo
            (Edo city). In: *Proc. 20th ISPRS Congress*. Ed. by A. Gruen, S. Murai,
            T. Fuse, and F. Remondino. International Archives of Photogrammetry,
            Remote Sensing and Spatial Information Sciences. 2004. URL: http:
            //www.isprs.org/proceedings/XXXVI/5-W1/papers/21.pdf [see pp.
            54, 65].

[GT14]   Girres, J.-F. and Touya, G. Cartographic generalisation aware of multi-
            ple representations. In: *Proc. 8th International Conference on Geographic*
            Information Science (GIScience). Ed. by M. Duckham, K. Stewart, and
            E. Pebesma. Poster. 2014 [see pp. 2, 51].

[GS01]   Gotsman, C. and Surazhsky, V. Guaranteed intersection-free polygon
            morphing. In: *Computers & Graphics* 25.1 (2001), pp. 67–75. DOI: 10.
            1016/S0097-8493(00)00108-4 [see pp. 53, 59, 65, 66].

[GH98]   Greiner, G. and Hormann, K. Efficient clipping of arbitrary polygons.
            In: *ACM Transactions on Graphics* 17.2 (1998), pp. 71–83. DOI: 10/
            bm9qsg [see p. 77].

[HSH04]   Hampe, M., Sester, M., and Harrie, L. Multiple representation databases
            to support visualization on mobile devices. In: *Proc. 20th ISPRS Con-*
            gress. Vol. XXXV (B4: IV). International Archives of Photogrammetry,
            Remote Sensing and Spatial Information Sciences. 2004, pp. 135–140.
            URL: http://citeseerx.ist.psu.edu/viewdoc/summary?doi=10.1.1.184.
            3303 [see pp. 51, 85].

[Har99]   Harrie, L. The constraint method for solving spatial conflicts in car-
            tographic generalization. In: *Cartography and Geographic Information*
            Science 26.1 (1999), pp. 55–69. DOI: 10.1559/152304099782424884
            [see pp. 3, 86].

[HS02]   Harrie, L. and Sarjakoski, T. Simultaneous graphic generalization of
            vector data sets. In: *GeoInformatica* 6.3 (2002), pp. 233–261. DOI: 10.
            1023/A:1019765902987 [see pp. 87, 90].

[HSD15]   Harrie, L., Stigmar, H., and Djordjevic, M. Analytical estimation of map
            readability. In: *ISPRS International Journal of Geo-Information* 4.2
            (2015), pp. 418–446. DOI: 10.3390/ijgi4020418 [see p. 17].

[HB03]   Harrower, M. and Brewer, C. A. Colorbrewer.org: An online tool for
            selecting colour schemes for maps. In: *The Cartographic Journal* 40.1
            (2003), pp. 27–37. DOI: 10.1179/000870403235002042 [see p. 111].

[HNR68]   Hart, P. E., Nilsson, N. J., and Raphael, B. A formal basis for the heuristic determination of minimum cost paths. In: *IEEE Transactions on Systems, Science, and Cybernetics* 4.2 (1968), pp. 100–107. DOI: 10.1109/TSSC. 1968.300136 [see pp. 4, 23].

[Hau05]   Haunert, J.-H. Link based conflation of geographic datasets. In: *Proc. 9th ICA Workshop on Generalisation and Multiple Representation (ICA-GM)*. 2005. URL: http://www1.pub.informatik.uni-wuerzburg.de/ pub/haunert/pdf/HaunertMapGen05.pdf [see p. 53].

[Hau09]   Haunert, J.-H. Aggregation in map generalization by combinatorial optimization. PhD thesis. Leibniz Universität Hannover, Germany, 2009. URL: https://dgk.badw.de/fileadmin/user_upload/Files/DGK/docs/c-626.pdf [see p. 37].

[HDO09]   Haunert, J.-H., Dilo, A., and van Oosterom, P. Constrained set-up of the tGAP structure for progressive vector data transfer. In: *Computers and Geosciences* 35.11 (2009), pp. 2191–2203. DOI: 10.1016/j.cageo.2008. 11.002 [see p. 11].

[HM16]   Haunert, J.-H. and Meulemans, W. Partitioning polygons via graph augmentation. In: *Proc. 9th International Conference on Geographic Information Science (GIScience)*. Ed. by A. J. Miller, D. O'Sullivan, and N. Wiegand. Vol. 9927. Lecture Notes in Computer Science. 2016, pp. 18–33. DOI: 10.1007/978-3-319-45738-3_2 [see p. 3].

[HS08]   Haunert, J.-H. and Sester, M. Assuring logical consistency and semantic accuracy in map generalization. In: *Photogrammetrie Fernerkundung Geoinformation* 2008.3 (2008), pp. 165–173. URL: https://www.dgpf. de/pfg/2008/pfg2008_3_Haunert.pdf [see pp. 3, 47].

[HW10a]   Haunert, J.-H. and Wolff, A. Area aggregation in map generalisation by mixed-integer programming. In: *International Journal of Geographical Information Science* 24.12 (2010), pp. 1871–1897. DOI: 10/c8v8s2 [see pp. 3, 12, 17, 37].

[HW10b]   Haunert, J.-H. and Wolff, A. Optimal and topologically safe simplification of building footprints. In: *Proc. 18th ACM SIGSPATIAL International Conference on Advances in Geographic Information Systems (ACMGIS)*. Ed. by A. E. Abbadi, D. Agrawal, M. Mokbel, and P. Zhang. 2010, pp. 192–201. DOI: 10.1145/1869790.1869819 [see pp. 4, 68].

[HW16]   Haunert, J.-H. and Wolff, A. Räumliche Analyse durch kombinatorische Optimierung. In: *Handbuch der Geodäsie (6 Bände)*. Ed. by W. Freeden and R. Rummel. Springer Reference Naturwissenschaften. 2016, pp. 1–39. DOI: 10.1007/978-3-662-46900-2_69-2 [see pp. 3, 47].

[HW17]   Haunert, J.-H. and Wolff, A. Beyond maximum independent set: an ex-
           tended integer programming formulation for point labeling. In: *ISPRS
           International Journal of Geo-Information* 6.11 (2017). DOI: 10.3390/
           ijgi6110342 [see pp. 3, 29, 47].

[HS92]   Hershberger, J. and Snoeyink, J. Speeding up the Douglas–Peucker line-
           simplification algorithm. In: *Proc. 5th International Symposium on Spa-
           tial Data Handling (SDH)*. 1992, pp. 134–143. URL: http://citeseerx.
           ist.psu.edu/viewdoc/summary?doi=10.1.1.17.6932 [see p. 60].

[Hua+17]   Huang, L., Ai, T., van Oosterom, P., Yan, X., and Yang, M. A matrix-based
           structure for vario-scale vector representation over a wide range of map
           scales: the case of river network data. In: *ISPRS International Journal
           of Geo-Information* 6.7 (2017). DOI: 10.3390/ijgi6070218 [see p. 2].

[II88]   Imai, H. and Iri, M. Polygonal approximations of a curve—formulations
           and algorithms. In: *Machine Intelligence and Pattern Recognition*. Ed. by
           G. T. Toussaint. Vol. 6. Computational Morphology: A Computational
           Geometric Approach to the Analysis of Form. 1988, pp. 71–86. DOI:
           10.1016/B978-0-444-70467-2.50011-4 [see pp. 69, 75].

[Jar30]   Jarník, V. O jistém problému minimálním [About a certain minimal
           problem]. In: *Práce Moravské přírodovědecké společnosti* 6.4 (1930), pp.
           57–63 [see p. 6].

[Jia15]   Jiang, B. The fractal nature of maps and mapping. In: *International
           Journal of Geographical Information Science* 29.1 (2015), pp. 159–174.
           DOI: 10.1080/13658816.2014.953165 [see p. 113].

[Joh14]   Johnson, A. *Clipper—an open source freeware library for clipping and
           offsetting lines and polygons*. Accessed: 2017-08-22. 2014. URL: http:
           //www.angusj.com/delphi/clipper.php [see p. 79].

[Kar84]   Karmarkar, N. A new polynomial-time algorithm for linear program-
           ming. In: *Combinatorica* 4.4 (1984), pp. 373–395. DOI: 10/czqmxn
           [see p. 28].

[Kea75]   Keane, M. The size of the region-building problem. In: *Environment
           and Planning A: Economy and Space* 7.5 (1975), pp. 575–577. DOI: 10.
           1068/a070575 [see p. 16].

[Koc88]   Koch, K.-R. *Parameter Estimation and Hypothesis Testing in Linear Mod-
           els*. Springer-Verlag New York, Inc., 1988. DOI: 10.1007/978-3-662-
           03976-2 [see p. 4].

[KS06]   Kokholm, N. and Sestoft, P. *The C5 Generic Collection Library for C#
           and CLI*. IT University of Copenhagen, 2006. URL: https://www.itu.
           dk/research/c5/ [see p. 100].

[Kre01]   van Kreveld, M. Smooth generalization for continuous zooming. In: *Proc. 5th ICA Workshop on Generalisation and Multiple Representation (ICAGM)*. 2001. URL: http://www.staff.science.uu.nl/~kreve101/papers/smooth.pdf [see pp. 1, 51, 86].

[Kru56]   Kruskal, J. B. On the shortest spanning subtree of a graph and the traveling salesman problem. In: *Proceedings of the American Mathematical Society* 7.1 (1956), pp. 48–50. DOI: 10.2307/2033241 [see p. 6].

[LL00]   Latecki, L. J. and Lakamper, R. Shape similarity measure based on correspondence of visual parts. In: *IEEE Transactions on Pattern Analysis and Machine Intelligence* 22.10 (2000), pp. 1185–1190. DOI: 10.1109/34.879802 [see p. 87].

[Lea92]   Leach, G. Improving worst-case optimal delaunay triangulation algorithms. In: *Proc. 4th Canadian Conference on Computational Geometry (CCCG)*. 1992. URL: http://citeseerx.ist.psu.edu/viewdoc/summary?doi=10.1.1.56.2323 [see p. 101].

[LW80]   Lee, D. T. and Wong, C. K. Quintary trees: a file structure for multidimensional datbase sytems. In: *ACM Transactions on Database Systems* 5.3 (1980), pp. 339–353. DOI: 10.1145/320613.320618 [see p. 98].

[Li+17]   Li, J., Ai, T., Liu, P., and Yang, M. Continuous scale transformations of linear features using simulated annealing-based morphing. In: *ISPRS International Journal of Geo-Information* 6.8 (2017). DOI: 10.3390/ijgi6080242 [see pp. 2, 67].

[LLX17]   Li, J., Li, X., and Xie, T. Morphing of building footprints using a turning angle function. In: *ISPRS International Journal of Geo-Information* 6.6 (2017). DOI: 10.3390/ijgi6060173 [see pp. 2, 68].

[LGC13]   Li, W., Goodchild, M. F., and Church, R. An efficient measure of compactness for two-dimensional shapes and its application in regionalization problems. In: *International Journal of Geographical Information Science* 27.6 (2013), pp. 1227–1250. DOI: 10/c5kg [see p. 17].

[LZ12]   Li, Z. and Zhou, Q. Integration of linear and areal hierarchies for continuous multi-scale representation of road networks. In: *International Journal of Geographical Information Science* 26.5 (2012), pp. 855–880. DOI: 10.1080/13658816.2011.616861 [see p. 2].

[LM17]   Lubiw, A. and Mondal, D. On compatible triangulations with a minimum number of steiner points. In: *Proc. 29th Canadian Conference on Computational Geometry (CCCG)*. 2017, pp. 101–106. URL: http://arxiv.org/abs/1706.09086 [see p. 66].

[Lue78]   Lueker, G. S. A data structure for orthogonal range queries. In: *Proc. 19th Annual Symposium on Foundations of Computer Science (SFCS)*. 1978, pp. 28–34. DOI: 10.1109/SFCS.1978.1 [see p. 98].

[Mac85]   Maceachren, A. M. Compactness of geographic shape: Comparison and evaluation of measures. In: *Geografiska Annaler: Series B, Human Geography* 67.1 (1985), pp. 53–67. DOI: 10/c329 [see p. 17].

[MBD16]   Mackaness, W. A., Burghardt, D., and Duchêne, C. Map generalization. In: *International Encyclopedia of Geography: People, the Earth, Environment and Technology.* 2016, pp. 1–16. DOI: 10/cx89 [see p. 1].

[Mas06]   Masuyama, A. Methods for detecting apparent differences between spatial tessellations at different time points. In: *International Journal of Geographical Information Science* 20.6 (2006), pp. 633–648. DOI: 10/c9k3jg [see p. 97].

[MD10]   Maus, A. and Drange, J. M. All closest neighbors are proper delaunay edges generalized, and its application to parallel algorithms. In: *Norsk Informatikkonferanse.* Ed. by T. Fallmyr and E. Hjelmås. 2010, pp. 1–12. URL: http://heim.ifi.uio.no/~arnem/Nik2010/PaperLatex.pdf [see p. 100].

[Mei16]   Meijers, M. Building simplification using offset curves obtained from the straight skeleton. In: *Proc. 19th ICA Workshop on Generalisation and Multiple Representation (ICAGM).* 2016. URL: https://kartographie. geo.tu-dresden.de/downloads/ica-gen/workshop2016/genemr2016_paper_11.pdf [see p. 71].

[MSO16]   Meijers, M., Savino, S., and van Oosterom, P. SPLITAREA: An algorithm for weighted splitting of faces in the context of a planar partition. In: *International Journal of Geographical Information Science* 30.8 (2016), pp. 1522–1551. DOI: 10.1080/13658816.2016.1140770 [see p. 13].

[MN07]   Midtbø, T. and Nordvik, T. Effects of animations in zooming and panning operations on web maps: a web-based experiment. In: *The Cartographic Journal* 44.4 (2007), pp. 292–303. DOI: 10/dgnjmj [see pp. 1, 111].

[MH16]   Minas, J. P. and Hearne, J. W. An optimization model for aggregation of prescribed burn units. In: *TOP* 24.1 (2016), pp. 180–195. DOI: 10. 1007/s11750-015-0383-y [see p. 17].

[Mul91]   Muller, J.-C. Generalization of spatial databases. In: *Geographical Information Systems: Principles and Applications.* Ed. by D. J. Maguire, M. F. Goodchild, and D. W. Rhind. 1991, pp. 457–475 [see p. 88].

[Mül+95]   Müller, J.-C., Weibel, R., Lagrange, J.-P., and Salgé, F. Generalization: State of the art and issues. In: *GIS and Generalization: Methodology and Practice.* Ed. by J.-C. Müller, J.-P. Lagrange, and R. Weibel. GISDATA 1. 1995. Chap. 1, pp. 3–17 [see p. 1].

[MD08]   Mustière, S. and Devogele, T. Matching networks with different levels of detail. In: *GeoInformatica* 12.4 (2008), pp. 435–453. DOI: 10.1007/s10707-007-0040-1 [see p. 55].

[Nöl+08]   Nöllenburg, M., Merrick, D., Wolff, A., and Benkert, M. Morphing poly-lines: A step towards continuous generalization. In: *Computers, Environment and Urban Systems* 32.4 (2008), pp. 248–260. DOI: 10/c7fgrw [see pp. 2, 4, 51, 52, 54, 56, 67, 85, 88, 92, 97].

[OH17]   Oehrlein, J. and Haunert, J.-H. A cutting-plane method for contiguity-constrained spatial aggregation. In: *Journal of Spatial Information Science* 15 (2017), pp. 89–120. DOI: 10.5311/JOSIS.2017.15.379 [see pp. 4, 12, 35, 49].

[Oos95]   van Oosterom, P. The GAP-tree, an approach to On-the-Fly map generalization of an area partitioning. In: *GIS and Generalization: Methodology and Practice*. Ed. by J.-C. Mueller, J.-P. Lagrange, and R. Weibel. 1995, pp. 120–132 [see pp. 51, 85].

[Oos05]   van Oosterom, P. Variable-scale topological data structures suitable for progressive data transfer: The GAP-face tree and GAP-edge forest. In: *Cartography and Geographic Information Science* 32.4 (2005), pp. 331–346. DOI: 10/chr7sf [see pp. 11, 12, 22, 47, 51, 85].

[OM14]   van Oosterom, P. and Meijers, M. Vario-scale data structures supporting smooth zoom and progressive transfer of 2D and 3D data. In: *International Journal of Geographical Information Science* 28.3 (2014), pp. 455–478. DOI: 10.1080/13658816.2013.809724 [see pp. 2, 12].

[Oos+14]   van Oosterom, P., Meijers, M., Stoter, J., and Šuba, R. Data structures for continuous generalisation: tGAP and SSC. In: *Abstracting Geographic Information in a Data Rich World: Methodologies and Applications of Map Generalisation*. Ed. by D. Burghardt, C. Duchêne, and W. Mackaness. Lecture Notes in Geoinformation and Cartography. 2014. Chap. 4, pp. 83–117. DOI: 10.1007/978-3-319-00203-3_4 [see p. 12].

[OS95]   van Oosterom, P. and Schenkelaars, V. The development of an interactive multi-scale GIS. In: *International Journal of Geographical Information Systems* 9.5 (1995), pp. 489–507. DOI: 10/fgzjvb [see p. 13].

[PH15]   Palfrader, P. and Held, M. Computing mitered offset curves based on straight skeletons. In: *Computer-Aided Design and Applications* 12.4 (2015), pp. 414–424. DOI: 10/c5zd [see p. 77].

[Pan+09]   Pantazis, D., Karathanasis, B., Kassoli, M., Koukofikis, A., and Stratakis, P. Morphing techniques: Towards new methods for raster based cartographic generalization. In: *Proc. 24th International Cartographic Conference (ICC)*. 2009. URL: https://icaci.org/files/documents/ICC_proceedings/ICC2009/html/refer/19_5.pdf [see p. 51].

[PS82]   Papadimitriou, C. H. and Steiglitz, K. *Combinatorial Optimization: Algorithms and Complexity*. Dover Books on Computer Science Series. Dover Publications, 1982 [see p. 4].

[Pat]   Patel, A. Amit's A* Pages. Accessed: Jul 26, 2018. URL: http://theory.
            stanford.edu/~amitp/GameProgramming [see p. 23].

[PDZ12]   Peng, D., Deng, M., and Zhao, B. Multi-scale transformation of river
            networks based on morphing technology. In: *Journal of Remote Sensing*
            16.5 (2012), pp. 953–968. URL: http://www.jors.cn/jrs/ch/reader/
            view_abstract.aspx?file_no=r11272&flag=1 [see pp. 2, 51, 85].

[Pen+13]   Peng, D., Haunert, J.-H., Wolff, A., and Hurter, C. Morphing polylines
            based on least squares adjustment. In: *Proc. 16th ICA Workshop on Gen-
            eralisation and Multiple Representation (ICAGM)*. 2013. URL: https://
            kartographie.geo.tu-dresden.de/downloads/ica-gen/workshop2013/
            genemappro2013_submission_6.pdf [see pp. 9, 51, 59, 67].

[PT17]   Peng, D. and Touya, G. Continuously generalizing buildings to built-
            up areas by aggregating and growing. In: *Proc. 3rd ACM SIGSPATIAL
            Workshop on Smart Cities and Urban Analytics (UrbanGIS)*. 2017. DOI:
            10.1145/3152178.3152188 [see p. 8].

[PW14]   Peng, D. and Wolff, A. Watch your data structures! In: *Proc. 22nd An-
            nual Conference of the GIS Research UK (GISRUK)*. Ed. by J. Drummond.
            2014, pp. 371–381. URL: https://www.gla.ac.uk/media/media_
            401742_en.pdf [see p. 9].

[PWH16]   Peng, D., Wolff, A., and Haunert, J.-H. Continuous generalization of
            administrative boundaries based on compatible triangulations. In: *Proc.
            19th AGILE Conference on Geographic Information Science, Geospatial
            Data in a Changing World*. Ed. by T. Sarjakoski, Y. M. Santos, and T. L.
            Sarjakoski. Lecture Notes in Geoinformation and Cartography. 2016,
            pp. 399–415. DOI: 10/c5kh [see pp. 8, 67, 97].

[PWH17]   Peng, D., Wolff, A., and Haunert, J.-H. Using the A* algorithm to find
            optimal sequences for area aggregation. In: *Proc. 28th International
            Cartographic Conference (ICC), Advances in Cartography and GIScience*.
            Ed. by M. P. Peterson. Lecture Notes in Geoinformation and Cartogra-
            phy. 2017, pp. 389–404. DOI: 10.1007/978-3-319-57336-6_27 [see
            pp. 7, 45, 67].

[Poh73]   Pohl, I. The avoidance of (relative) catastrophe, heuristic competence,
            genuine dynamic weighting and computational issues in heuristic prob-
            lem solving. In: *Proc. 3rd International Joint Conference on Artificial In-
            telligence (IJCAI)*. 1973, pp. 12–17. URL: https://exhibits.stanford.
            edu/feigenbaum/catalog/sq127cx4634 [see p. 24].

[Pri57]   Prim, R. C. Shortest connection networks and some generalizations. In:
            The Bell System Technical Journal 36.6 (1957), pp. 1389–1401. DOI:
            10.1002/j.1538-7305.1957.tb01515.x [see pp. 6, 74].

[Rad+89]   Rada, R., Mili, H., Bicknell, E., and Blettner, M. Development and application of a metric on semantic nets. In: *IEEE Transactions On Systems Man And Cybernetics* 19.1 (1989), pp. 17–30. DOI: 10.1109/21.24528 [see pp. 37, 38].

[RKW13]   Rahmati, Z., King, V., and Whitesides, S. Kinetic data structures for all nearest neighbors and closest pair in the plane. In: *Proc. 29th Annual Symposium on Computational Geometry (SoCG)*. 2013, pp. 137–144. DOI: 10.1145/2462356.2462378 [see p. 100].

[Reg01]   Regnauld, N. Contextual building typification in automated map generalization. In: *Algorithmica* 30.2 (2001), pp. 312–333. DOI: 10.1007/s00453-001-0008-8 [see pp. 3, 5, 68, 72].

[RR07]   Regnauld, N. and Revell, P. Automatic amalgamation of buildings for producing ordnance survey 1:50 000 scale maps. In: *The Cartographic Journal* 44.3 (2007), pp. 239–250. DOI: 10.1179/000870407x241782 [see p. 68].

[RI04]   Reilly, D. F. and Inkpen, K. Map morphing: making sense of incongruent maps. In: *Proc. Graphics Interface (GI)*. Ed. by W. Heidrich and R. Balakrishnan. 2004, pp. 231–238. URL: https://dl.acm.org/citation.cfm?id=1006086 [see p. 51].

[Rui+11]   Ruiz, J. J., Ariza, F. J., Ureña, M. A., and Blázquez, E. B. Digital map conflation: a review of the process and a proposal for classification. In: *International Journal of Geographical Information Science* 25.9 (2011), pp. 1439–1466. DOI: 10.1080/13658816.2010.519707 [see p. 97].

[Saa85]   Saalfeld, A. A fast rubber-sheeting transformation using simplicial coordinates. In: *The American Cartographer* 12.2 (1985), pp. 169–173. DOI: 10/cs5dt3 [see p. 53].

[Saa88]   Saalfeld, A. Conflation automated map compilation. In: *International Journal of Geographical Information Systems* 2.3 (1988), pp. 217–228. DOI: 10.1080/02693798808927897 [see p. 98].

[Saa99]   Saalfeld, A. Topologically consistent line simplification with the Douglas–Peucker algorithm. In: *Cartography and Geographic Information Science* 26.1 (1999), pp. 7–18. DOI: 10/drcc5h [see pp. 13, 53, 63, 66].

[Saf+13]   Safra, E., Kanza, Y., Sagiv, Y., and Doytsher, Y. Ad hoc matching of vectorial road networks. In: *International Journal of Geographical Information Science* 27.1 (2013), pp. 114–153. DOI: 10.1080/13658816.2012.667104 [see p. 97].

[SH15]   Schneider, T. and Hormann, K. Smooth bijective maps between arbitrary planar polygons. In: *Computer Aided Geometric Design* 35–36 (2015), pp. 243–354. DOI: 10.1016/j.cagd.2015.03.010 [see p. 51].

[Sch86]   Schrijver, A. *Theory of Linear and Integer Programming*. John Wiley &
             Sons, Inc., 1986. URL: https://promathmedia.files.wordpress.com/
             2013/10/alexander_schrijver_theory_of_linear_and_integerbookfi-
             org.pdf [see p. 5].

[Sch+13]   Schwartges, N., Allerkamp, D., Haunert, J.-H., and Wolff, A. Optimizing
             active ranges for point selection in dynamic maps. In: *Proc. 16th ICA
             Workshop on Generalisation and Multiple Representation (ICAGM)*. 2013.
             URL: https://kartographie.geo.tu-dresden.de/downloads/ica-gen/
             workshop2013/genemappro2013_submission_5.pdf [see p. 4].

[Sch95]   Schwarzkopf, O. The extensible drawing editor Ipe. In: *Proc. 11th An-
             nual Symposium on Computational Geometry (SCG)*. 1995, pp. 410–411.
             DOI: 10.1145/220279.220326 [see p. 111].

[Sed+93]   Sederberg, T. W., Gao, P., Wang, G., and Mu, H. 2-D shape blending: An
             intrinsic solution to the vertex path problem. In: *Proc. 20th Annual Con-
             ference on Computer Graphics and Interactive Techniques (SIGGRAPH)*.
             1993, pp. 15–18. DOI: 10.1145/166117.166118 [see p. 87].

[SB04]   Sester, M. and Brenner, C. Continuous generalization for fast and smoo-
             th visualization on small displays. In: *Proc. 20th ISPRS Congress*. Ed.
             by O. Altan. Vol. XXXV (Part B4). International Archives of the Pho-
             togrammetry, Remote Sensing and Spatial Information Sciences. 2004,
             pp. 1293–1298. URL: http://citeseerx.ist.psu.edu/viewdoc/summary?
             doi=10.1.1.67.9129 [see pp. 51, 85].

[Ses00]   Sester, M. Generalization based on least squares adjustment. In: *Proc.
             19th ISPRS Congress*. Ed. by D. Fritsch and M. Molenaar. Vol. XXXIII
             (Part B4). International Archives of Photogrammetry and Remote Sens-
             ing. 2000, pp. 931–938. URL: http://www.isprs.org/proceedings/
             Xxxiii/congress/part4/931_XXXIII-part4.pdf [see pp. 87, 90].

[Ses05]   Sester, M. Optimization approaches for generalization and data abstrac-
             tion. In: *International Journal of Geographical Information Science* 19.8–
             9 (2005), pp. 871–897. DOI: 10.1080/13658810500161179 [see p. 3].

[SB05]   Sester, M. and Brenner, C. Continuous generalization for visualization
             on small mobile devices. In: *Proc. 11th International Symposium on Spa-
             tial Data Handling (SDH)*. Ed. by P. Fisher. 2005, pp. 355–368. DOI:
             10.1007/3-540-26772-7_27 [see p. 2].

[SH75]   Shamos, M. I. and Hoey, D. Closest-point problems. In: *Proc. 16th An-
             nual Symposium on Foundations of Computer Science (SFCS)*. 1975, pp.
             151–162. DOI: 10.1109/SFCS.1975.8 [see p. 98].

[SH76]   Shamos, M. I. and Hoey, D. Geometric intersection problems. In: *Proc.
             17th Annual Symposium on Foundations of Computer Science (SFCS)*.
             1976, pp. 208–215. DOI: 10.1109/SFCS.1976.16 [see p. 99].

[Shi05]   Shirabe, T. A model of contiguity for spatial unit allocation. In: *Geographical Analysis* 37.1 (2005), pp. 2–16. DOI: 10.1111/j.1538-4632. 2005.00605.x [see p. 35].

[Sma03]   van Smaalen, J. Automated Aggregation of Geographic Objects. PhD thesis. Wageningen University, 2003 [see pp. 12, 49].

[Smi+07]   Smith, G., Beare, M., Boyd, M., Downs, T., Gregory, M., Morton, D., Brown, N., and Thomson, A. UK land cover map production through the generalisation of OS MasterMap®. In: *The Cartographic Journal* 44.3 (2007), pp. 276–283. DOI: 10.1179/000870407X241827 [see p. 13].

[Sto+09a]   Stoter, J., van Smaalen, J., Bakker, N., and Hardy, P. Specifying map requirements for automated generalization of topographic data. In: *The Cartographic Journal* 46.3 (2009), pp. 214–227. DOI: 10/fttg54 [see p. 2].

[Sto+09b]   Stoter, J. et al. Methodology for evaluating automated map generalization in commercial software. In: *Computers, Environment and Urban Systems* 33.5 (2009). Geo-information Generalisation and Multiple Representation, pp. 311–324. DOI: 10.1016/j.compenvurbsys.2009. 06.002 [see pp. 73, 76].

[Str00]   Streinu, I. A combinatorial approach to planar non-colliding robot arm motion planning. In: *Proc. 41st Annual Symposium on Foundations of Computer Science (FOCS)*. 2000, pp. 443–453. DOI: 10.1109/SFCS. 2000.892132 [see p. 87].

[Šub+16]   Šuba, R., Driel, M., Meijers, M., Eisemann, E., and van Oosterom, P. Usability test plan for truly vario-scale maps. In: *Proc. 19th ICA Workshop on Generalisation and Multiple Representation (ICAGM)*. 2016. URL: http: //www.gdmc.nl/publications/2016/Usability_Test_Plan_Vario-scale_ Maps.pdf [see p. 111].

[ŠMO16]   Šuba, R., Meijers, M., and van Oosterom, P. Continuous road network generalization throughout all scales. In: *ISPRS International Journal of Geo-Information* 5.8 (2016). DOI: 10.3390/ijgi5080145 [see pp. 1, 2].

[SG01]   Surazhsky, V. and Gotsman, C. Controllable morphing of compatible planar triangulations. In: *ACM Transactions on Graphics* 20.4 (2001), pp. 203–231. DOI: 10.1145/502783.502784 [see p. 53].

[SG03]   Surazhsky, V. and Gotsman, C. Intrinsic morphing of compatible triangulations. In: *International Journal of Shape Modeling* 09.02 (2003), pp. 191–201. DOI: 10.1142/S0218654303000115 [see p. 59].

[SG04]   Surazhsky, V. and Gotsman, C. High quality compatible triangulations. In: *Engineering with Computers* 20.2 (2004), pp. 147–156. DOI: 10/ c7hfws [see p. 59].

[TS18]   Thiemann, F. and Sester, M. An automatic approach for generalization
            of land-cover data from topographic data. In: *Trends in Spatial Analy-
            sis and Modelling: Decision-Support and Planning Strategies*. Ed. by M.
            Behnisch and G. Meinel. Vol. 19. Geotechnologies and the Environment.
            2018. Chap. 10, pp. 193–207. DOI: 10/c5kj [see p. 13].

[Tim98]   Timpf, S. Hierarchical Structures in Map Series. PhD thesis. Technical
            University Vienna, Austria, 1998. URL: http://citeseerx.ist.psu.edu/
            viewdoc/download?doi=10.1.1.62.4561&rep=rep1&type=pdf [see p.
            12].

[Ton+15]   Tong, X., Jin, Y., Li, L., and Ai, T. Area-preservation simplification of
            polygonal boundaries by the use of the structured total least squares
            method with constraints. In: *Transactions in GIS* 19.5 (2015), pp. 780–
            799. DOI: 10.1111/tgis.12130 [see p. 3].

[TLJ14]   Tong, X., Liang, D., and Jin, Y. A linear road object matching method
            for conflation based on optimization and logistic regression. In: *Inter-
            national Journal of Geographical Information Science* 28.4 (2014), pp.
            824–846. DOI: 10.1080/13658816.2013.876501 [see p. 97].

[TP66]   Töpfer, F. and Pillewizer, W. The principles of selection. In: *The Carto-
            graphic Journal* 3.1 (1966), pp. 10–16. DOI: 10.1179/caj.1966.3.1.10
            [see pp. 81, 84, 113].

[TD17]   Touya, G. and Dumont, M. Progressive block graying and landmarks en-
            hancing as intermediate representations between buildings and urban
            areas. In: *Proc. 20th ICA Workshop on Generalisation and Multiple Rep-
            resentation (ICAGM)*. 2017. URL: https://kartographie.geo.tu-dresden.
            de / downloads / ica - gen / workshop2017 / genemr2017_paper_1.pdf
            [see pp. 2, 68, 111].

[TG13]   Touya, G. and Girres, J.-F. ScaleMaster 2.0: A ScaleMaster extension to
            monitor automatic multi-scales generalizations. In: *Cartography and
            Geographic Information Science* 40.3 (2013), pp. 192–200. DOI: 10.
            1080/15230406.2013.809233 [see p. 12].

[Vat92]   Vatti, B. R. A generic solution to polygon clipping. In: *Communications
            of the ACM* 35.7 (1992), pp. 56–63. DOI: 10/ct78wx [see p. 79].

[Vol06]   Volz, S. An iterative approach for matching multiple representations of
            street data. In: *Proc. Joint ISPRS Workshop on Multiple Representations
            and Interoperability of Spatial Data*. 2006, pp. 101–110 [see p. 97].

[Wei97]   Weibel, R. Generalization of spatial data: Principles and selected al-
            gorithms. In: *Algorithmic Foundations of Geographic Information Sys-
            tems*. Ed. by M. van Kreveld, J. Nievergelt, T. Roos, and P. Widmayer.
            Vol. 1340. Lecture Notes in Computer Science. 1997. Chap. 5, pp. 99–
            152. DOI: 10.1007/3-540-63818-0_5 [see pp. 1, 68].

[WB17]   Weibel, R. and Burghardt, D. Generalization, on-the-fly. In: *Encyclope-dia of GIS*. Ed. by S. Shekhar, H. Xiong, and X. Zhou. 2nd ed. 2017, pp. 657–663. DOI: 10.1007/978-3-319-17885-1_450 [see p. 1].

[WR09]   Whited, B. and Rossignac, J. B-morphs between b-compatible curves in the plane. In: *Proc. 2009 SIAM/ACM Joint Conference on Geometric and Physical Modeling*. Ed. by W. F. Bronsvoort, D. Gonsor, W. C. Regli, T. A. Grandine, J. H. Vandenbrande, J. Gravesen, and J. Keyser. 12. 2009, pp. 187–198. DOI: 10.1145/1629255.1629279 [see p. 87].

[WR11]   Whited, B. and Rossignac, J. Ball-morph: Definition, implementation, and comparative evaluation. In: *IEEE Transactions on Visualization and Computer Graphics* 17.6 (2011), pp. 757–769. DOI: 10.1109/TVCG. 2010.115 [see pp. 2, 59].

[Wil09]   Williams, H. P. *Logic and Integer Programming*. 1st ed. Springer, 2009. DOI: 10.1007/978-0-387-92280-5 [see p. 29].

[Wil02]   Williams, J. C. A zero-one programming model for contiguous land acquisition. In: *Geographical Analysis* 34.4 (2002), pp. 330–349. DOI: 10.1111/j.1538-4632.2002.tb01093.x [see p. 35].

[WRC83]   Wright, J., Revelle, C., and Cohon, J. A multiobjective integer program-ming model for the land acquisition problem. In: *Regional Science and Urban Economics* 13.1 (1983), pp. 31–53. DOI: 10/dqgvs5 [see p. 17].

[WSM04]   Wu, S.-T., da Silva, A. C. G., and Márquez, M. R. G. The Douglas–Peucker algorithm: Sufficiency conditions for non-self-intersections. In: *Journal of the Brazilian Computer Society* 9.3 (2004), pp. 67–84. DOI: 10/cxwv [see p. 13].

[Xia13]   Xia, G. The stretch factor of the delaunay triangulation is less than 1.998. In: *SIAM Journal on Computing* 42.4 (2013), pp. 1620–1659. DOI: 10.1137/110832458 [see p. 101].

[You88]   Young, H. P. Measuring the compactness of legislative districts. In: *Leg-islative Studies Quarterly* 13.1 (1988), pp. 105–115. DOI: 10.2307/ 439947 [see p. 17].

[ZM08]   Zhang, M. and Meng, L. Delimited stroke oriented algorithm-working principle and implementation for the matching of road networks. In: *Geographic Information Sciences* 14.1 (2008), pp. 44–53. DOI: 10.1080/ 10824000809480638 [see p. 97].

[ZS83]   Zoltners, A. A. and Sinha, P. Sales territory alignment: a review and model. In: *Management Science* 29.11 (1983), pp. 1237–1256. DOI: 10. 1287/mnsc.29.11.1237 [see p. 34].

Acknowledgments

Obtaining a Ph.D. in Germany was one of the best things I could dream of. When I finally got the chance to study in Germany, I was thrilled and I wanted to do my best. Now I feel so proud of myself because I have come this far. Of course, this dissertation would not have been possible if it were not for the help of many people.

First of all, I would like to thank my first supervisor, Prof. Dr. Alexander "Sascha" Wolff. I am grateful to him for giving me the opportunity to pursue my Ph.D. in his group. The research work was challenging, but I enjoyed working with him. Sascha has been very patient with me. When I first came to Germany, I could barely speak English. He had to put a lot of effort into understanding me when we were doing research. Sascha advised me to take lectures and sent me to conferences so that I could learn as much as possible. Sascha always encouraged me to ask questions because I can benefit from the answers. He told me not to be shy even when I fear that the questions are stupid; other people in the audience may appreciate my asking because they may have the same questions but don't dare to ask. At some point, Sascha even negotiated with my landlords when I moved from an apartment into another. Moreover, Sascha has a good sense of humor, and we often cracked jokes together. I was lucky to have him as my supervisor.

I also thank my second supervisor, Prof. Dr. Jan-Henrik Haunert. In his lecture *Algorithms for GIS*, he taught me many fundamentals of GIScience. Later, he moved to other universities and invited me to visit him there. During the visits, we sketched many ideas together. In particular, he proposed using the A^* algorithm to find optimal sequences for area aggregation, which led to the most important chapter of my dissertation. Furthermore, he recommended many suitable conferences to me when I wanted to publish my papers.

I am grateful to all the colleagues in our group: Moritz Beck, Johannes Blum, Benedikt Budig, Steven Chaplick, Thomas van Dijk, Martin Fink, Oksana Firman, Krzysztof Fleszar, Philipp Kindermann, Myroslav Kryven, Fabian Lipp, Andre Löffler, Nadine Schwartges, Joachim Spoerhase, Sabine Storandt, and Johannes Zink. We often had coffees together, and it was a lot of fun to play squash and to go out for our excursions. It was nice that our group always had lunch together so that we had plenty of chances to learn from each other. Indeed, I sometimes took advantage of these lunches to get suggestions regarding my research work. I am also grateful to Sigrid Keller. She found an apartment for me before I arrived in Germany. Then, she picked me up at the train station of Würzburg and brought me to that apartment. She was very kind to me and helped me to fill many forms related to my Ph.D. study.

I am indebted to Dr. Krzysztof Fleszar for helping me a lot during my Ph.D. study. He is very warm-hearted. Whenever he found that I had problems to understand a paper, he read that paper and then explained it to me. He always helped when I needed a German–English translator. He helped me move twice using the van of his family. On the day before my defense, he worked as hard as me in order to give me feedback about my slides. He has always invited me to join his parties, which brought me many great times.

I thank Dr. Guillaume Touya for inviting me to visit the French National Mapping Agency (IGN). The visit was a great chance and gave me insight into practical requirements regarding maps. Our collaboration resulted in a paper on continuously generalizing buildings into built-up areas. I also thank Dr. Thomas van Dijk. He helped me speed up my least-squares adjustment using *Eigen*, a C++ library. He has proofread some of my papers and has given me helpful suggestions concerning many aspects of my research.

I am grateful to Prof. Dr. Min Deng, the supervisor of my master's study. He introduced me into the research area of continuous map generalization and helped me to get the chance of pursuing my Ph.D. at the University of Würzburg. Under his supervision, we coauthored some nice papers.

I thank Prof. Dr. Dirk Burghardt for reviewing my dissertation within a short time frame when my working contract in Würzburg was about to end. I also thank him for introducing my research work to Prof. Dr. Peter van Oosterom, which certainly helped me to get a postdoc position in Peter's group. Before submitting the final version of my dissertation, I have already been working in Peter's group. I would like to thank Peter and Dr. Martijn Meijers for allowing me to finish my paper about area aggregation, which is part of this dissertation.

I would like to thank my parents for all their love and encouragement. I thank them for their suggestions when I was making decisions. I thank all my friends in Würzburg for their company. Because of them, I could better explore the city and even the whole country.

I am very grateful to the University of Würzburg, which is a treasure trove of knowledge. I had the opportunity to take many courses. In order to gain sufficient credits for obtaining a Ph.D. degree in Computer Science, I took some courses (e.g., *Theoretical Computer Science* and *Algorithms and Data Structures*) in my own faculty, the Faculty of Mathematics and Computer Science. In order to improve my language skills, I took many courses offered by the Language Center (e.g., *English for the Natural Sciences* and *General Language Exercise of German*) and by the Faculty of Arts (e.g., *Introduction to English Linguistics*).

The reviewers of my dissertation were Prof. Dr. Alexander Wolff and Prof. Dr. Dirk Burghardt. I defended my dissertation on December 21, 2017. The defense examiners were Prof. Dr. Andreas Nüchter (chair), Prof. Dr. Jan-Henrik Haunert, and Prof. Dr. Alexander Wolff.

Curriculum Vitae

 Dongliang Peng was born on October 26, 1987 in Yonghe, Liuyang, Changsha, Hunan, China. In 2009, he obtained his bachelor's degree in Mapping Engineering at Central South University (CSU), Changsha, China. His bachelor's thesis is entitled "Updating Geographical Data based on AutoCAD". He continued to study Cartography and Geographic Information Engineering at CSU. In 2012, he obtained his master's degree with thesis "A Methodology of Morphing Transformation of Linear Features for Map Continuous Generalization". Both the bachelor's and master's theses were under the supervision of Prof. Dr. Min Deng.

From 2012 to 2017, he pursued his Ph.D. degree in Computer Science at Julius Maximilian University of Würzburg (JMU), Germany. The title of his dissertation is "An Optimization-Based Approach for Continuous Map Generalization", which was supervised by Prof. Dr. Alexander Wolff and Prof. Dr. Jan-Henrik Haunert.

Since 2018, he became a postdoctoral researcher in Section of GIS Technology, Delft University of Technology (TU Delft), The Netherlands. He works with Prof. Dr. Peter van Oosterom and Dr. Martijn Meijers on the topic of vario-scale maps.

www.ingramcontent.com/pod-product-compliance
Lightning Source LLC
LaVergne TN
LVHW080117070326
832902LV00015B/2637